REM
W EXFORD

REMEMBERING
WEXFORD

Nicky Rossiter

The
History
Press
Ireland

Remembering Wexford is dedicated primarily to the two grandchildren who have arrived since the earlier publications – Jack and Jude.

It is also, of course, for Ellie, Finn, Lola and Ziggy, in the hope of inspiring them to continue the task in the future.

Also for Mark, David, Kate and Paula.

Without Anne it would never have been completed – thanks yet again.

It is also published in memory of Katie and Nicky.

First published 2010

The History Press Ireland
119 Lower Baggot Street
Dublin 2, Ireland
www.thehistorypress.ie

© Nicky Rossiter, 2010

The right of Nicky Rossiter to be identified as the Author
of this work has been asserted in accordance with the
Copyrights, Designs and Patents Act 1988.

British Library Cataloguing in Publication Data.
A catalogue record for this book is available from the British Library.

ISBN 978 1 84588 993 7

Typesetting and origination by The History Press
Printed in Great Britain
Manufacturing managed by Jellyfish Print Solutions Ltd

CONTENTS

INTRODUCTION

Welcome to the final part of a quartet of my books on Wexford published by Nonsuch/The History Press Ireland. It has been fascinating to have a chance not only to look back on this town, but to share it with so many readers at home and abroad. Modern communication has offered us the oppurtunity to get feedback on our efforts which has been an added bonus. In this book I have included some of that feedback.

When we look at the volume of information that we have researched, written and published on this one medium-sized town in the corner of Ireland, we have to wonder whether Wexford is unique in that it can produce so much history or whether there is an ever-yawning void to be filled by the local historians of all those other towns.

The transport in this picture dates it to perhaps the early 1940s. Beyond the cyclist, the 'corporation man' is busy with his street sweeping, using the double dustbin on wheels. Hairdressing businesses seem popular on this section of street, with Kirwan's on the right and another barber's pole up near the corner of Bride Street. Mann's Lane looks even narrower than in later times. (Courtesy of Kiernan/Scanlon Collection)

Dating from the early 1900s, this shows the sign for the YMCA on the light outside the premises on the left.

Perhaps to the dismay of some readers, I have generally stayed within 'the ring road' of Wexford and more specifically concentrated on the Wexford that thrived before Kennedy Park, Bernadette Place and Newtown Road beyond 'the monument'. This was a conscious decision, because I do not have as much knowledge of the areas beyond those boundaries. In addition, if I had included even the surrounding villages I would be writing for a lifetime.

Remembering Wexford is a curious exercise. The bulk of the book is taken up with personal recollections of the town and its environs over the past few decades. But like all such recollections, they spark further thoughts and the research leads us to other items that are important, relevant or just plain fascinating. Because of this,

I decided not to restrict myself to things that reside in my memory alone. I have included some interesting items reflecting life in Wexford over about a century. I have always been fascinated by how crimes and corporations were reported in the past – it is one of the book proposals that I haven't followed up (yet) – and I include a few examples here.

The bibliography lists the sources of many of the items included. These range from printed books, to unpublished works, to personal letters and emails. In particular I thank Sylvia and Jimmy O'Connor for permission to quote once again from some unpublished but very well-researched work and the use of some of their photographs. They have been a constant source of research material, pictorial and otherwise, in these books and articles going back a few decades now.

Once again I must express my gratitude to Dominic Kiernan for providing some excellent photographs from the Kiernan/Scanlon Collection, and acknowledge the foresight and photographic expertise of the late John Scanlon that allowed these visual treasures to be preserved and shared with the present generation.

While every effort has been taken to ascertain and fully acknowledge the sources of photographs, anecdotes and other material, we apologise for any omissions and if alerted we will rectify the matter in any future editions.

My thanks to Ronan and the staff at The History Press Ireland for putting up with the queries during the process of creating this book and organising the launch.

ANNE STREET REVISITED

I am grateful to John E. Sinnott for sending me extra information on Anne Street following the publication of *The Streets of Wexford*. John describes the street a few decades ago as follows.

On the south side there was The Lamb House owned by Con Collins. Next came a lane that serviced Harry Stone's and The Gas Company. This is probably the current rear exit for The Book Centre, which now occupies the former Harry Stone's premises.

Here we have the old Boggan's Garage on the quay, with the solitary petrol pump on the kerb. Imagine a car trying to pull in to fill up in such a location today. (Rossiter Collection)

John recalled Foxes public house, where they also ran a hackney business. This was later Pierce Roche's and featured fictionally in Billy Roche's excellent novel of Wexford called *Tumbling Down*. It later became Meyler's and I spent many an evening in Anne Street drinking Club Orange with Leo Murphy in a Morris Minor with the registration number AMI 4. This would be a treat following an early start that morning, travelling to the fish market in Dublin with the Wexford catch.

This was the quay-side entrance to John English & Co. Founded by John English in the early 1900s in premises on the corner of Anne Street and Commercial Quay, English's specialised in high-class printing and hand-crafted bookbinding and it also supplied pen-ruled ledger books to local businesses. (Courtesy of Kiernan/Scanlon Collection)

Sonny Clancy's Butcher Shop was in the porch of Clancy's Hotel, which we later knew as The County Hotel, with its glass porch awning. Then there was Boggan's Garage, from where the bus service operated.

There was a lane servicing the hotel and Mamie Scalon had a second-hand furniture store there. Lambert's Bakery was also located in the lane. This lane may have joined Cullimore's Lane, stretching from near The Crescent to Main Street, emerging between what John recalls as Nolan's, later Healy & Collins (finally Dunne's) and Devereux's, later the L&N Tea Company (now Euro 2). John calls Slegg's Lane 'Skinyard Lane', and mentions it exiting under Curran & Walls shop, later Arthur Kelly's.

On Anne Street there was a long and high stone wall opposite the post office and behind was the Bond Store. He was aware of 'a smashing apple tree' there too. There was an office beside the wall probably connected to the Bond Store. Then came what he calls a 'big house' and then Hopkins's and Busher's Garage. These ran hackney cars and he believes they also owned a fishing boat. The two garages on Anne Street had petrol pumps on the footpath. Then came the bank yard, bank house and the bank.

On the opposite side, starting again at Main Street, was Lambert's house. Then, after a short wall, came the bakery flour store. John recalls a man running pongo sessions in the store at a later date. It was called Knoxies. I remember this store from my time working in Joyce's as their store for gas cylinders among other items. One of the delivery men for those cylinders was Des Waters, the actor, director and chronicler of the city of Taghmon. The store had a basement area and it was connected to an iron cover in the footpath where coke was delivered for the bakery.

Next came a lane that serviced Lambert's, Bessie O'Connor's, Pat Whelan's, Kehoe's Shoe Shop, Rochford's (later Pat Whelan's Irish House) and Foxe's Sweet Shop. Then came what John calls 'the Baptist church'. After a space was and still is the post office. The Wexford Club came after the lane that still leads into Church Lane. It was at another time called The Gentlemen's Club. The old Labour Exchange was next. My recollection of this building was as another store for Joyce's. On the corner was English's printing works with living quarters above.

CLONARD

Wexford has been expanding rapidly throughout the past century. In my lifetime there were just green fields beyond Browne's pub, and quite an amount of greenery within that boundary. Today there are housing developments out to the ring road and beyond.

Perhaps the most significant development in this sphere has been the Clonard/ Coolcotts area, where a whole new parish had to be developed in a location that already had a history but was rather sparsely populated even into the later decades of the twentieth century.

Coolcotts is the older of the two names associated with the area. It has at least two possible interpretations from the Gaelic. Coill na Coitte or the 'wood of the cotts', denotes a wood where timber was grown for use in the construction of boats called cotts. The other was Cúl Cotts, 'the back of Kaat's', meaning behind Van Kaat's shipyard at Westgate. The latter is perhaps the more fanciful. Clonard is a name common to many towns in Ireland. It is usually translated as 'the high meadow' and is a topographical feature.

In researching the history of this parish and its people in times past, we come across a number of interesting connections.

The house on the south-east Abbey Street corner, formerly the Central Police Barracks and later Miss Beirne's Girls' School, was built by Madame Hatton of Clonard, who also owned Great Clonard and Little Clonard. She was a sister of Lord Castlereagh of the Union.

At Coolcotts in 1809, a meadow of three-and-a-half acres lately owned by Pat Furlong of Cornmarket was to let. It was noted in the advertisement in the *Wexford Herald* as 'situated half a mile from town on the road to Seaview'.

Animal theft was said to be increasing in 1808, with reports of 'a fat pig stolen from a woman in the Faith and a ram taken off Philip Doyle's land at Coolcotts where it was skinned and the carcass taken'.

In 1831, an epidemic called 'hooping' (probably whooping) cough was reported in the *Wexford Independent*. Three daughters of James Stafford of Coolcotts are reported to have died and been buried in one grave.

Belvedere Road was noted as opposite Airhill. It was said to be the road to a sand pit and brick kiln in 1880. In 1891, there was a newspaper advertisement for 'Best bricks for sale, Mr Malone of Belvidere'. This probably refers to Belvedere House, which is still standing in the area. Incidentally the older spelling is more accurate in its descriptive use, meaning 'lovely view', and the house does look down over Wexford to the harbour.

Left: Now housing an interpretive centre as well as housing units, in the late 1900s the yard at Westgate was primarily used for parking and storage. The stalls had housed horses and carts prior to motorised transport. (Kiernan/ Scanlon Collection)

Below: Located on Belvedere Road, Hadden's was a well known furniture factory in the mid-twentieth century. The premises was later subdivided into units and housed a plumbing supply company and a photo processors. It was subsequently demolished and used for a housing development. (Rossiter Collection)

This area at the south end of Wexford under Batt Street and Maudlintown is generally referred to as the Cott Safe. It was a haven for the small rowing or sailing boats of the local population, who used them for leisure and maybe a bit of fishing. It was also used for regattas, which were regular features of town life in the 1950s and before. (Rossiter Collection)

Clonard House was for sale in 1894, located on fifty-five acres of watered and timbered land, giving an indication of the sparse habitation a century ago. It was listed as consisting of a drawing room, dining room, parlour, five principal bedrooms, servants' rooms, WC, and a basement suitable for cellars. It had a garden with greenhouse, peach house and vinery and orchard, surrounded by a high wall. There were stables for eight horses as well as loose boxes, a coach house, oat lofts, hay shed for 100 tons, four houses for forty head of cattle, a dairy and a piggery. The house was approached by gate entrance with a gate lodge. Clonard was listed as being situated two English miles from Wexford. The sale was conducted by Walsh & Son auctioneers for William Browne.

The so-called Paupers Graveyard is in Coolcotts Lane. Only one headstone exists with an inscription, that of John Brien, who died 2 December 1904, aged twelve. The other burials are not marked and are believed to be those of inmates of the workhouse.

Early in the 1900s, a company purchased land at Clonard from St Peter's College. It was enclosed and levelled. A handball alley with seating for 400 was built, as was a cricket pitch, a football ground, a running track and a stand to hold 600 spectators. This, the new Wexford Park, also had provision for show-jumping and agricultural shows. Some years later, in 1912, an air show was staged in the park, and a plane actually took off from there, only to lose power and crash at the Cott Safe off Batt Street.

In 1939, Wexford County Council raised a loan of £1,200 from the National Bank to strengthen and surface road from the urban boundary at Belvedere via Wexford Sports Field to Clonard.

Coolcotts Lane had a dispensary in 1940.

In 1969, Wexford Corporation sold land in the Clonard area for the building of a church for the rapidly growing population. The land was sold for £2,800.

In 1974, a new parish of Clonard was created due to the rising numbers of residents.

CROMWELL'S FORT

For many years one of the iconic symbols of the merchant princes of Wexford had to be Cromwell's Fort. In the mid-twentieth century it was home to the Stafford family, whose presence was to be felt in shipping, coal distribution, retail sales and many other spheres of our lives.

The irony is that for Wexford the name Cromwell had always been anathema. He was recalled solely for the slaughter of innocent people and religious intolerance, but here was one of the pre-eminent families living in a house apparently named after him.

The general consensus, however, is that the house does not commemorate the person, but rather the area on which it was built. Tradition has it that the Cromwellian troops set up guns at Trespan, from where they shelled the castle. Cromwell's Fort was built on land adjoining the rocks. Dan Walsh also considers the name as descriptive of 'sloping wood', which it certainly was, but what a coincidence if the description and the location of the guns were the same. Still, one must wonder at the decision for the original name and its continued use even into the present day in connection with houses on the land.

This interesting photograph shows what is probably the management of a number of the Stafford enterprises preparing for an outing. The picture was taken on South Main Street and shows three of the shops. (Courtesy of Kiernan/Scanlon Collection)

This is one of the Stafford's Shops at Stonebridge. It would later be converted to give us the Capitol Cinema and the Granada Grill.

The original house was built in the 1780s for Isaac Cornock, who was a descendant of Captain Cornock, who had arrived here with Cromwell in 1649. Revd Zachariah Cornock lived there in 1837 and it was still in Cornock hands up to at least 1913, albeit through John Hawkes-Cornock.

James J. Stafford purchased the house and lands in 1915, when he came to prominence as owner of such enterprises as J.J. Stafford & Co., Wexford Timber Company, and Wexford Steamship Company. His son, also James J., was prominent in business as well and was made a Knight of St Gregory by Pope Pius XII. His wife Colleen was deeply involved in the early years of Wexford Festival Opera and entertained many celebrities at the house.

Although we always viewed Cromwell's Fort as a mansion, it appears to have had only eight bedrooms, some large reception areas and a marble hall. Big when compared to the normal two-up two-down that most were familiar with, but not the aristocratic residence we all thought.

I recall having attended school in The Presentation in the 1950s with one of the sons of the Stafford family, but the occasional meeting in a classroom is all I can remember. Their house was surrounded by a high wall; you could not even really see the house from the road and there were the usual tales of gamekeepers and dogs to keep you well away from it.

The house was eventually sold to a developer in 1995, and with the main house converted to apartments, the lands would accommodate numerous small estates of houses, all recalling Cromwell, either the man or the sloping wood.

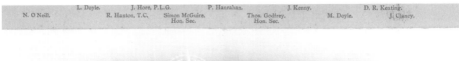

N. O'Neill.   L. Doyle.   J. Hore, P.L.G.   P. Hanrahan.   J. Kenny.   D. R. Keating.
R. Hanton, T.C.   Simon McGuire.   Thos. Godfrey.   M. Doyle.   J. Clancy.
Hon. Sec.   Hon. Sec.

J. Stafford, Ald.   B. Hughes, T.C.,   P. Ryan,   H. McGuire, Ald.,   E. O'Connor.
Hon. Treas.   Vice-Pres.   Mayor, Pres.   Vice-Pres.
N. J. Cosgrave, H.C.   P. Byrne.   Jas. Lee.

C. E. VIZE,   WEXFORD.

Wexford Boro' '98 Association.----Committee.

Above: Commemoration Committee, 1798. This photograph, taken by Charles Vize, epitomises the era of the change from the nineteenth to the twentieth centuries. The participants – all male – represent the business and political structure of the time. Note the formal posing and the stern looks. (Courtesy of O'Connor Collection)

Left: Green Street was named after John Green, who was mayor of Wexford seven times. He championed the idea of piped water. Our picture shows the ever popular Bolger's shop where pupils of the CBS spent their pennies. (Courtesy of Jim Bergin Collection)

ENTERTAINMENT

Few things can spur our memories of the past like recalling how we spent our spare time. A few decades ago, instead of television, PlayStations or Sky Plus, we looked to live shows.

In 1961, Mandrake the Magician was advertised as playing at the Dun Mhuire. This may have been a sort of touring version of a popular cartoon character which appeared in the newspapers such as the *Evening Herald*. It may even have been our first unknowing view of a franchise.

Tops of the Town were staged for the first time in Wexford in 1962. This gave local factories and businesses a new way of competing. The shows were a great mixture of variety acts, all performed in those early days by actual employees of the firms or relatives or friends. As time went on they added guest stars, sometimes professionals, and competed for the national finals with television appearances. But in those early years they held us spellbound over the weeks of Lent when dancing was prohibited. Inter-firm competition raged with great intensity. The shows gave rise to a number of entertainment icons for Wexford, such as Toddy Rossiter, John Hayes and Slim Redmond as ballet stars in *The People* Newspaper Show.

This is the Crescent before the development of the Mall of Henrietta Street or Donovan's Wharf. In the left foreground is the derelict sawmill that earned the nickname of 'The Hippy Hotel' in the Festival of Living Music in 1971. The building to the right of the John Barry statue was a forge and later a second-hand book store called Bookends. (Rossiter Collection)

Bingo arrived at Dun Mhuire in 1963. The Dungeon Theatre Club opened under Ted Doyle's, North Main Street, in 1965. It later became The Playhouse.

But the entertainment was not all local or parochial. In 1970, the pop fans could see Edison Lighthouse live at Dun Mhuire. Michael Mc Liammorr appeared in The Theatre Royal. The Dun Mhuire also hosted Love Affair, The American Drifters, The Tremeloes (obviously after their Brian Poole days) costing 10s, and later in the year, Slim Whitman. Roger Whittaker was on stage in Enniscorthy and they also offered Professional Wrestling.

The first Wexford Festival of Living Music occurred in 1970 and the international artistes appearing included: Tara Telephone, Danny Doyle, Gay & Terry Woods, Fairport Convention, B.P. Fallon, St Sepulchre's Consort, Thin Lizzy, The Hennesseys. The bishop was the patron and the committee included Frank Sinnott, Philip Molloy, Dara Conneely and Lorcan Ennis.

The Crescent is reputedly the former Deep Pool of Wexford, which was used as a safe haven to carry out repairs to ships. This picture gives a good idea of how it looked prior to the removal of the Woodenworks and installation of the current quay front. (Rossiter Collection)

Miss Hot Pants 1971 was chosen at the Talbot Hotel, winning a holiday in Butlin's Holiday Camp at Mosney.

In that same year, Prophet Records, a new record company, was launched in Wexford by Larry Kirwan and Pierce Turner. Its releases were to be distributed by Polydor Records. The first release was by The Menapia Folk and featured a Turner/ Kirwan song, 'Bitter Whiskey, Sweet Red Wine'. The record moguls would later spread their wings more as performers, moving on to New York and greater things, but they remain faithful to their Wexford roots with regular local shows even to this day.

Those were also the days of the showbands, and Wexford was well served by such local groups. The Supreme Showband, also known as The Supreme Seven, even got on to vinyl with a song called 'Can't Go Back to Boston', with 'The Big Bamboo' on the flip side. There were also The Travellers, The Kinsellas or Kinsella Country, Mule, and a number of other outfits playing the halls at the time.

During Wexford Opera Festival in 1972, Josef Locke appeared at The Talbot Hotel, as did Anna McGoldrick and Sean Dunphy. The Gay Byrne radio show was also broadcast from Wexford at that time.

In 1973, Herman's Hermits topped the bill at the Dun Mhuire, while Mungo Jerry was at Whites Hotel with a cover charge of 50p. The same admission got you in to the band Christie when they were on stage at Whites Barn.

In 1975, Joseph Locke was back, but this time in the Dun Mhuire. The folk diva Julie Felix appeared in Whites Barn in the same year. Helen Shapiro also starred there, with a 75p admission. Later in the year, Sandie Shaw was at Whites, and Val Doonican was in the Dun Mhuire costing £1.50 a ticket. On a local note, Packy Hayden was advertised to appear on *The Late Late Show* on television. Marianne Faithful was in the Talbot Hotel in 1976, The Boomtown Rats were advertised for the Dolphin Bar in Maudlintown, and Billy J. Kramer was billed for Butlers of Broadway.

The following year saw Red Hurley at the Talbot Hotel, Marmalade at Whites Barn and Makem & Clancy in the Dun Mhuire. Later in the year, Dick Emery appeared in the Dun Mhuire, Kenneth McKeller in Whites Hotel and Paul Goldin was in Enniscorthy.

THE FREE PRESS

The very title of just 'The Free Press' reminds us of how local and rather isolated the towns of the mid-twentieth century were. We did not need to indicate this was a Wexford publication, just as The Wexford People was then simply The People and we had The Echo & South Leinster Advertiser rather than an array of town-designated titles.

My association with The Free Press at 59 South Main Street began, as so many sources of employment did in those days, with family connections rather than an advertised vacancy and interviews. My mother had worked for the company before her marriage and as always in that era parents were on the lookout for a good trade for their offspring and so she kept in touch with old friends and contacts in what was then seen as one of the good trades to be in.

What we often forget is the pace of change that has occurred in half a century, especially in the media. Although I entered the front door of The Free Press less than fifty years ago, the trade and the premises of that and many other such firms was only a step on from Dickensian times. However, things would change at breakneck speed over coming years.

The Free Press was a newspaper and 'general jobbing house' printers based on South Main Street. Entry for the workers at the time was via a hall door at number 59 and, unusual as it may seem today, the staff would gather there for admission by the foreman each morning and lunchtime.

The premises consisted of a large townhouse of three floors through which the operatives passed to reach a back door and passage with old converted outhouses on one side leading to the main works. The Main Street building housed management, the Corcoran brothers who owned the business, the reporting staff and the office staff.

The office staff, George Kingsbury and Ann Kavanagh, were the frontline workers for the paper for most people. In the large office behind a high counter and often sitting on high wooden stools, they dealt with the many personal notices that were the lifeblood of a newspaper. These were death notices, anniversaries, acknowledgements, novenas, petitions, lost and found, situations vacant and wanted, and a load of other categories. There were also the people coming in to purchase papers and to have 'wrapped papers' sent to friends and relatives abroad. This was a service whereby as soon as a newspaper was printed (well, next day really) the staff wrapped it securely, attached a label and stamp and posted it to the addressee. Some people probably didn't trust the system so they bought wrapped papers and sent them on, while other more canny customers got a paper and a wrapper and added a personal letter before despatching the local news to London, Liverpool, New York or elsewhere.

George was also the advertising agent who visited businesses to procure the bigger advertisements, and more importantly, to chase up payments. The office staff also proofread the advertisements and sometimes the copy, as well as the material from the general jobbing section.

The reporters were ensconced upstairs. There was an editor and two or three reporters. In the early days a Mr Cruise O'Brien edited the paper – before my time. Mr Cronin was also slightly before my time. Jim Finnerty was editor at one stage and he oversaw the transition to news on the front page. The first front-page news in a Wexford newspaper appeared in *The Free Press* in March 1969. In earlier times all newspapers, including the nationals, had advertising on the front page. It changed earlier for national newspapers, but the provincial papers, as the locals were called, held on to that tradition much longer. *The Free Press* was the first in Wexford to change.

Other reporters that I recall on *The Free Press* were Dermot Walsh, Brendan Furlong and Peter Doyle. After editing newspapers Dermot went on to public relations and to write a number of books of national interest. Brendan also went into the editor's seat and he continues to write for local and national titles. Peter, who is a cousin of mine, was most famous in *The Free Press* for his show-business column (we envied the freebies) and he too went onward and upward to an editor's position.

Accessing the printing works from the public office, you went down what may once have been an alley. For the most part it was covered in my time with racks containing reams of paper on the right-hand side. On the left were whitewashed walls of old sheds. In some of these there was more paper storage.

In another of these, John Flaherty had his workplace. John had primary responsibility for 'setting up' the newspaper. He worked on the newspaper all week and other compositors only began to assist him as the deadline approached. These included Dermot Kelly, Michael Carthy, Eugene Robinson and Ian Lawlor. Much of the newspaper content stayed static over periods. Repeat advertisements were held over from previous weeks. The basic composition of other pieces was retained; for example, cinema advertising was a block of type with some permanent lines and the others changed with the week's attractions. Another staple of provincial newspapers were the non-news items, which ranged from cookery columns to looking back a hundred years at old news stories. These were essential because they could be prepared weeks in advance. They kept the compositors – as John Flaherty would be known – busy in the early days of the week, otherwise it could have meant days with nothing to do and then a hectic few days as news stories were written.

In fact, provincial newspapers were not prone to cries of 'hold the front page' as they only contained advertising anyway. News trickled in and if it came too late there was no sense of urgency. There would be another edition next week.

Corporation meetings were usually held on Monday nights, giving plenty of time to write up the reports. Court reports were another staple of coverage, along with sports stories. With most sporting events at weekends, again there was no urgency. Deaths and obituaries were also not matters of rushing to print.

Approaching the red door to the printing works, there was a corrugated iron shed to the right. Here Ibar Fortune had the task of melting down the old used type and preparing ingots of metal to feed the linotype machines. The type was melted down in an old gas-fired pot, with God knows what type of emissions. The only ventilation came from the fact that the shed was open at the top and bottom on the one exposed wall.

Entering through that red door brought you into the bowels of *The Free Press*. In a large warehouse-type structure that appeared to have been a large yard that had been covered in with a big glass section in the roof that allowed in natural daylight, you found a huge paper guillotine, various printing machines, metal tables, stacks of paper and two pot-bellied stoves. One stove, just inside that door, and another in the middle of a works area that was about 150 yards by 50 yards and twenty-five-feet high to a partial glass roof were the extent of the heating in 1967, apart from a few strategically placed paraffin and bottled-gas heaters, which were jealously guarded by those senior enough to merit them. The responsibility of cleaning out and lighting the temperamental stoves rested with the apprentices. This was a mad idea because the two youngest arrivals were the least competent at getting the temperamental stoves up and running. It was usually only with the expertise of old hands like Ibar or Tom Mahon that some semblance of heat was coaxed from them. More often than not they produced more smoke than heat.

In printing, then, there were two separate and distinct trades. The compositors basically assembled the type and the printers printed the items. I was a printer. In those days you certainly started at the bottom and the bottom in *The Free Press* was a room to the left of the entrance door. In here were two machines called 'Arabs' – don't ask me why. These were the sort of machines you sometimes saw in cowboy films. In fact, viewers of *Larkrise to Candleford* will have seen a similar apparatus. This would have brought older print workers a smile, as it could never produce the newspaper it purported to do. At the cutting edge of technology, pulleys from a central shaft near the ceiling powered our two machines. An electrically driven motor in turn powered the shaft. A large foot pedal originally – and still in times of power cuts – powered the machines. To print on these machines you needed concentration and dexterity. These were hand fed. You picked up a sheet with your right hand, placed it on guides on a moving bed and plucked printed sheets off with your left hand. Sounds easy? This had to be done in fluid motion as tons on metal swished and moved. There certainly was an art to that kind of printing. Try lifting single sheets from a stack of paper without taking doubles. This sheet then had to sit perfectly on three guides – usually slugs of metal pasted on to a sheet of paper gummed over a pad of more sheets on paper. Every sheet had to be in the same position and straight, or else the printed result was off line. As the blank sheet was lifted the printed sheet had to be grabbed and removed before the stroke could be completed. All the while you had to maintain an even flow of ink to give uniform coverage on all printed sheets.

The ink was spread on an ingenious metal plate that rotated on cogs while rollers made on the premises trundled over the plate, down the type and up again for more ink on each stroke. Needless to say these machines, where initially I met Tony Busher and Tommy Dempsey, were not part of the newspaper section. This was the mainly local jobbing section, where invitation cards, tickets, invoice books, silver circle cards, memory cards and other items for local individuals and businesses were printed. It was also where wedding invitations were printed with white or silver ink and a person also dusted them with silver powder to enhance the print.

Outside the Arab Room was a long flat-bed machine that was used in those early days to print part of the newspaper and some of the Arab operatives transferred to it later in the week. This was to supplement the larger Wharfedale machines that

Ibar Fortune and Tommy Dempsey at work in *The Free Press*. (Rossiter Collection)

Left: Mary Street was also called Chapel Lane. Raby's Barn became a coal yard and later a slaughter house. The Wexford Wheel & Carriage Works of J.J. Murphy was here in 1945 and in 1949 it was the proposed site for a swimming pool fed by John Street reservoir. (Rossiter Collection)

Below: How many people would ever consider that a little over half a century ago the timber for Wexford homes was not delivered by road or even railway, but by ship, directly to the front door of a retailer like McCormack's. (Rossiter Collection)

produced the bulk of the publication. This machine, which we operated in the main street in Wexford in the 1960s, would have been equally at home in Tombstone or Culver City when Wyatt Earp and Billy the Kid roamed the west.

The full newspaper at that time was printed as two broadsheet pages at a time, then two more printed on the reverse. These were then folded and the required number of four-page sections inserted to produce a full newspaper. Print day was Thursday and work started at 8.30a.m. and, as they say, finished when it finished for those directly involved in production and packing. One other product of the Wharfedale was the cinema posters. These were long narrow playbills that were pored over by all staff as they came off the press to see what entertainment options were there for next week. Tony Bolger and Tommy Carthy were the old hands at this technology and probably produced at a speed comparable to many mechanised machines elsewhere.

That is no to say that every part of the company was rooted in an earlier era. There were also some ultra modern – for the time – automatic printing machines. In the main these were used for the 'bread and butter' work. This was contract work for government publications and ranged from printing the old insurance cards (from an era when your 'stamp' in work was actually a stamp that the employer purchased and pasted to a collection card) to colour brochures on 'Sheep Scour' for the Department of Agriculture. All such publications carried an intriguing code that might read, '10,000 FP 12/67 G4'. This meant ten thousand copies were printed by *The Free Press* in December 1967 for Agriculture. Such print orders were despatched weekly by the lorry load to The Stationary Office, Beggar's Bush, Dublin, at a time when we only knew Beggar's Bush from the Danny Doyle hit 'Whiskey on a Sunday'. Nicky Lawlor, later joined by Tommy Dempsey and Tony Bolger, was the main man or 'The King' in this section.

In the late 1960s there were major changes afoot in the printing industry. AnCo was the abbreviation for An Chomhairle Oiliunna, the forerunner of Fás, and apprentice training was taking on new impetus. We had to keep a journal showing what we worked on each day – probably to get away from the old idea of apprentices as general dogsbodies. Then they introduced 'block release', whereby apprentices were sent to Cork for three months each year for more theoretical and academic training in such august surrounding as the Crawford School of Art.

In technology, matters were speeding ahead. A rotary press was installed to print the newspaper. There was a gradual change from letterpress to lithography, and computers of a very basic variety began to replace the old mechanical marvels the linotype machines. The maestros of the linotype had been Reggie Turner the elder and the younger, Johnny Roche, Jem Sinnott and Joe Moloney.

Sadly, *The Free Press* newspaper would flounder before all these innovations flourished. It produced a final edition dated Friday 12 February 1971.

Left: This remnant of the malting industry, Mill House, stood at Paul Quay until a few years ago. (Rossiter Collection)

Below: The North End Garage was on the site of the Selskar Ironworks. It was demolished to make way for Dunnes Stores. (Courtesy of Hurley Collection)

SOME OF THE INDUSTRIES

In the year that Mandrake the Magician appeared on stage at the Dun Mhuire and a plaque to the boxer Jem Roche was unveiled in the Bullring, Edelweiss Dairy Products set up a factory on the outskirts of Wexford. The base was Rockland's House, and in true Wexford tradition, we seldom (if ever) used the official name. To us it was the Cheese Factory. From those beginnings in October 1961, the factory grew and grew, with a few name changes included, but we still used the original.

This is a catalogue illustration of the famous Pierce fire fan that graced many an Irish home into the mid-1900s. (Rossiter Collection)

This picture shows part of the old Pierce's dating from the 1970s that few, other than those working there, would have seen. It was an area up towards the Mulgannon Road where various components were stored while waiting for shipment. (Rossiter Collection)

As Wexford Creamery, it produced quality cheeses like Wexford Cheddar. Then a whey products section was added. It later produced baby foods in the world-famous Cow & Gate stable and continues to offer steady employment decades on.

In 1887 there was mention of a Wexford man called Lett exporting mussels to North Wales. A century later, the same name was on the boxes of mussels but the market was worldwide. The family operated seven boats out of Wexford in the 1950s and were said to be the largest exporter of live eels in the United Kingdom at the time. It was while in Billingsgate Market selling eels that Laurence Lett was made aware of a shortage of mussels and fielded enquiries about the possibility of any being available in Wexford. By 1963, the company was harvesting wild mussels in the Wexford area but with growing demand they moved into cultivating their own stock. To cover the off-season for mussels, they also harvested and supplied prawns and scampi.

Left: Monck Street takes its name from General Monck, who was granted the land and the ferry rights in the 1650s. It was previously known as Ferryboat Lane, from where the ferry to the opposite bank of the river departed prior to the construction of the 1794 bridge.

Below: The name Mulgannon was first cited in 1650. There was a reference to land at Roche's Town or the Moor Mulgannon in 1808. It was called the Duncormick Road in 1837. (Courtesy of Kiernan/Scanlon Collection)

How many of you recall a company with a product called Waico? Okay then, here's another clue – Brockhouse Industries. That will have stirred some memories with older readers no doubt. Then if we mention Waico Springs the penny will drop. It was established in Maudlintown in the 1930s and operated very successfully for about forty years. It later moved to part of the Pierce's complex.

We often forget that electricity is a relatively new power source. The general electrification of Wexford dates back only about a century. Prior to that, many large factories and enterprises generated their own private supplies. Before that we depended on gas for light, as well as for heat and cooking. The Wexford Gas Consumers Company started in Trinity Street in 1869. Just considering the extent of the network of safe solid piping that they had to install to supply their product to factories, homes and for street lighting, one must stand in awe of the undertaking. In addition, there were the logistics of lighting and extinguishing street lights every day of the year, as well as maintaining them. As the town expanded, the gas network also grew, with new housing estates being gas powered for cooking long after electricity took over in lighting (although I still recall gas lighting in a Wexford house as late as the 1960s).

The gasman was a familiar sight in all areas in the 1960s. He travelled by bicycle and had a leather satchel to carry the money. Today he would probably have a van with security guards. The reason for this collection was that gas was prepaid by meter. Every house had a little red box tucked away under the stairs. Into this went the sixpences or shillings needed to release the gas into the home to power the cooker. It was a constant vigil to ensure that there were enough coins available for the meter, otherwise there was no cooking. Christmas time was a killer for that small change. When the gasman came he emptied the meter, totted up the usage and sometimes there was a surplus to be handed back, due to variations in the tariff. You also got a receipt for the money collected.

In the 1970s there was consternation in Wexford as the Gas Company suddenly closed. Gas cookers had to be replaced. Government funding was needed to ease the burden and the matter eventually passed. Trinity Street lost the towering gasometers and new developments grew on the sites.

LOCAL GOVERNMENT

One thing I miss in local newspapers today is the almost verbatim reporting on Corporation meetings. Looking over a few random newspaper reports, we find how invaluable these are in recreating our town and its people. They show a town and population full of characters, sometimes with odd priorities but always great entertainment. The topics were often deadly serious and the points made were both valid and important, but looked at in hindsight, they could remind us of the fictitious Ballymagash.

ASSISTING TOURISTS

At a Wexford Corporation meeting, one of the councillors proposed that parking should be banned in front of the 1798 monument of the pike man in the Bullring. The reasoning was that tourists were prevented from 'getting a clear shot of it with vans, lorries and cars parked around it'. The Corporation agreed to bring this to the attention of the Gardaí.

GAS COOKERS ON LONG-TERM HIRE PURCHASE

At a Corporation meeting in 1973, there was a proposal that the 5p rental that had been added to local-authority tenants' rents to pay for gas cookers installed when they took up residence be removed. The reasoning was that after paying for twenty years, the cookers were well paid for. Ironically, the gas cookers would become obsolete a very short time later, with the demise of 'town gas'.

THE SHORTCUT

Back in 1945, there was an innovative idea floated in Wexford County Council based on a Wexford Corporation proposal. This suggested opening a 'shortcut' from Wexford to Rosslare across the South Slob, in particular for cyclists and pedestrians. The idea would have been a progression from a traditional water-based route. In times past, when a large proportion of inhabitants (particularly in the south end of town) had small boats or had friends or relatives with such vessels, it was common for them to row to Rosslare for an outing.

The Horse River, or Bishopswater River, passes behind the malt stores of Upper King Street known as the Pillar. (Courtesy of Kiernan/Scanlon Collection)

King Street Avenue is perhaps unknown to the majority of Wexford residents. It is accessed via a lane without a title going up beside the wall of the Pillar development. (Courtesy of Kiernan/ Scanlon Collection)

The proposal was not new, because as far back as 1926 about £2,000 had been spent on an approach road and an estimate of about £2,590 for its completion was made in 1942. The plan at that point was that the track would take cyclists, light traffic and farm carts. The erection of a necessary bridge over the existing railway line would increase the cost by another £2,000. Things were exacerbated because the railway company also wanted a rent of £100 per year. The land was owned by Meldon Estates. The county manager reported that not only did the railway company seek rent, but 'wanted them to keep a permanent man there'.

When asked if the track could accommodate cyclists, the county engineer made a rather interesting reply, 'Cyclists made a diversion through the fields because there was no bottom to the road.' After some discussion, it emerged that it was unlikely they would get funding and another innovative idea bit the dust.

BATTLE OF CLONTARF

Today people talk about the power or lack thereof of local government, especially the Corporation, or to give them their proper title, Wexford Borough Council. Looking at an old newspaper I was delighted to find an almost verbatim report on a meeting in 1914.

Bullring, in the early 70s. This Sunday morning shot reminds us of the popularity of the Mini at that time, along with the Morris Minor. Lambert's pub was still trading beside the market and Traynor's was on Main Street, where it would later be sold to the Northern Bank which in turn became National Irish Bank. The traditional cream and green telephone box had not given way to the Perspex ones. (Rossiter Collection)

Market in the Bullring on a summer Saturday. The van is selling strawberries as well as other farm produce. Diana Donnelly's, in the background, was a high-priced ladies' clothing store. It was located on the site of the birthplace of Oscar Wilde's mother, which had been a rectory at one time. (Courtesy of Kiernan/Scanlon Collection)

The Dublin Corporation wrote asking the council to appoint delegates to attend a meeting in Dublin to arrange for a fitting celebration of the 900th anniversary of the Battle of Clontarf:

Mayor: Will you appoint any delegates to attend?

Mr Byrne: I think it is hardly necessary. The battle happened a long time ago.

Alderman Kelly: I don't remember it anyhow. (Laughter)

Mr Byrne: Let any member who wishes attend.

Mr McMahon: I would like to see Wexford represented.

Mayor: But the proposed meeting is only to make arrangements for the celebration. I think Councillor McGuire's view of the matter is right, because, after all, you will have to leave it in the hands of the Dublin Corporation to make the necessary arrangements. Whenever the celebration takes place, then we will consider the advisability of sending representatives to it.

Will there be a celebration in 2014?

NICKNAMES

Nicknames sometimes seem to be a dying art. Just as the Christian names are following media trends, many modern nicknames tend to follow suit. In compiling this section there is a slight dilemma. Were the older names accepted, were they even known by all the recipients or were they found to be insulting? To steer clear of giving offence, perhaps were will avoid identifying the person if at all possible. The nicknames were often amusing. Then again some might have had deeper meanings but they did give a certain flavour to the period.

The Bullring to the Cornmarket. This shot, taken after the demolition of Sloan's, gives us a good view of Paddy Kelly's shop. It is also ideally dated by the posters for the infamous Festival of Living Music in 1971. (Courtesy of Kiernan/Scanlon Collection)

On Fridays and Saturdays the Bullring attracted a plethora of traders. One of the most interesting was 'Cheap Charlie', who sold all sorts of novelty items. He had a spiel not unlike Del Boy Trotter, including, 'I don't want a tenner, not even a fiver, missus, you can have the two for four quid' and, 'It's the change that breaks me.' (Courtesy of Kiernan/Scanlon Collection)

'Jinks' was the name given to one teacher, though the reason for that is unknown. Another teacher, this time of Latin, is more obvious in that he was 'Mensa' (the Latin for table I think, for those who were schooled after those classic education days). Yet another teacher was 'Hoss' and many believe this referred to his bulky resemblance to Hoss Cartwright in the TV show *Bonanza*. Yet another was 'The Bear' because he was a rather grizzly old character who grew grapes in a greenhouse at 'the monastery'. Of course there was the generic 'The Boss' for the principal. I suppose they all knew they had nicknames in some way and one can have little sympathy, because some of them were adept at christening others, like one teacher who referred to a pupil who walked with a stoop as 'Here's me head, me arse is coming'.

Some nicknames went automatically with surnames – or so it seemed to us. There was 'Block' Dempsey, 'Bardog' Roche and 'The Bull'. Then there were occupational ones, like 'The Dabber' for a painter, 'Stab the Rasher' for a grocer, 'Shilling a Stitch' for a dressmaker and 'Vistavision' for a cinema projectionist.

In work there was 'The Man' for the boss or foreman, and 'The King' for the person who saw the place as his domain. There was also 'Babóg', a name sometimes given to a young apprentice. 'Scootchie' was an awful-sounding nickname given to some people and it is hard to fathom why it was attached. The original scootch referred to propelling a boat on the sloblands.

In an article in *The Wexford Echo* a few years back, Nicky Furlong added greatly to our store of nicknames, with such wonderful nomenclatures as 'Six Eggs', 'Hairy Paw', 'No Stocking', 'Leg in the Hollow' (a bit cruel for one with a short leg; I recall some of us referring to person with an odd walk as 'Step in the Hollow'), 'Mug o' Tar' and 'Lourdes Water O'Neill' (a pious man doing his best to spread the faith).

These are supplemented by 'Whacker', 'Suck', 'Butch', 'Lordy', 'Basket Arse', 'The Camel', 'Little Da', 'Moll Trot', 'Duck' and 'Dooshie' (possibly a small person based on the adjective). Sadly the origins of some of these may never be revealed, either because they cannot be traced or for fear of libel. The article did reveal some of the more noteworthy people with nicknames, such as 'The Quavering Tenor' O'Neill, 'Hop the Cod' Furlong, 'The Midnight Milkman' (that is an intriguing one) and 'Sansa', along with 'Diddler Doyle' and 'Slippy Fippence'.

PARENTS

My memories of Wexford always revolve around family. Although I have been lucky enough to travel quite widely, I have always lived and worked in my hometown and was lucky enough to have a wide-ranging family always on hand to visit, even if in the younger days it was a bit of a chore.

In my youth we lived opposite my paternal grandparents, who were a refuge if I had been less than well behaved at home. My maternal grandfather lived with my aunt on Roche's Terrace and their house was a regular destination on Friday nights, where a 'three-penny bit' was the weekly reward. Aunt Kitty was the destination on Sunday mornings for many years, after Mass and before going to 'pay the society'. Other aunts and uncles lived in various parts of town and we paid regular visits. We also looked forward to the annual trips home each summer by aunts and uncles living abroad, as so many did in those years.

My mother, Katie was the source of many of the expressions in this book. She was pure Wexford and epitomised her generation. She left school early and worked in Cousin's mineral factory in St Peter's Square, only a few hundred yards from her family home. She later worked in *The Free Press*, which was a bit further away but not too much. In fact, if she had taken a circular route to and from work, she would only have walked 'round the block' – down Gibson's Lane to work, along South Main Street and up Bride Street to Roche's Terrace.

All too often we forget that our parents had real lives just as we do. They played games, they went to school, they dated, they were young newlyweds at one time. Unfortunately we seldom document or even hear the minutiae of those lives in Wexford before the Second World War that the majority of our parents lived. My mother probably spent fewer than five nights anywhere other than in her own bed. But her life was obviously full. No doubt as a young girl she played the games of the period on Roche's Terrace and probably in the grounds of Bride Street church.

Being a neighbourhood like most others, there were friends and relatives to visit within a few doors. Maggie Bergin lived a few doors away. I can only recall her as an older woman but apparently her husband was a very well-thought-of GAA player before his death at a young age. Next door lived the Healys. Paddy was a cobbler with a shop in Cornmarket. His wife was always known as Mag and her mother Bessie Crosbie lived with them and their sons John, Joe, Michael, Peter and Martin. Bessie was related to the famous Paddy and Martin Crosbie. The former was schoolteacher in Dublin synonymous with the long running radio and later television show *The School Around the Corner*. Martin was a singer who appeared regularly on radio and in the top theatres in the land, including the Theatre Royal

Named after Fr Roche, the driving force behind the twin churches, and dominated by the similarly titled Roche's Terrace, this picture of Roche's Road shows a time before television. There are no aerials or satellite dishes on view. It was from this terrace that I watched President Kennedy in 1963. (Courtesy of Kiernan/Scanlon Collection)

in Wexford. His wife Thelma was the accordion player on *The School Around the Corner*. The Dublin Crosbies often holidayed in Wexford. They were somehow related to us and I guess some of their singing talent migrated, because my uncle Peter and aunt Peggy were top turns for singing at family gatherings. Katie was pretty good too but was usually too shy to sing anywhere other than in the house.

Katie was not a drinker or smoker but probably enjoyed the odd night out at the pictures in one of the three cinemas within easy reach, with a few chips bought on the way home. Sunday outings would be to such exotic locations as Carrig Graveyard (made famous in the song 'Carrig River'), Browne's Bank off Maudlintown, and Jemmy William's Rock up Whiterock Hill.

We know that life in those decades was far from easy. She lost her brother Tommy and sister Alice to tuberculosis when they were young adults. She did not travel abroad but walked probably more than the circumference of the earth. Her routine was like clockwork. Five days every week she walked to 'ten Mass' in Bride Street church. She then went 'downtown' to do a few messages before heading home to make the dinner. This was dinner, not lunch. At about half past one she was again walking down Casa Rio, Distillery Road and King Street to Cullimore's, later Nancy Codd's bookie office to place bets for herself and a few of the neighbours and relations. She would then get a few more 'messages' – this was how people referred to doing the shopping. After that it was up to see Peggy, her sister, on Roche's Terrace and then home to get the racing results on BBC radio at about four thirty before making the tea.

Her evening vice was the bingo. Like so many housewives of the era, this was a major social outlet rather than a gambling sojourn, although they all bragged of 'sweating on one number for the hundred-pound jackpot'. The bingo was one activity that enticed Katie and many others out of Wexford. The main venues for bingo were Joe Dillon's, the Parish Hall and Fr Sinnott's, but there were also big games in Camross and Taghmon and these were reached by buses laid on by the venues. Such outings had the ladies of Bishopswater making new friends from

Behind the boat is the caravan and camping park and old swimming pool at Ferrybank. Before this was developed, the fields in that area were known as the Dairy Fields and this was a well-known and well-frequented location for courting couples. (Rossiter Collection)

around the county who were watched out for and worried about if they failed to get on the bus any particular week. The trips to bingo were as ritualised as any religious practice. There were bingo boards required to rest the books on, the bags of sweets for refreshment, the assorted markers and the few bob to buy chips at the break. There was also a sort of mutually agreed rule that if you won a few bob – and it was only a few shillings or pounds most times – you gave your friends a small share.

Katie lived life for her family and friends in her own town, with religion, shopping, chatting with friends and her bingo enough for a full and happy life. Ironically, for such a reluctant traveller, she died suddenly on a trip to pre-pilgrimage Our Lady's Island and was buried on what would have been her wedding anniversary.

The other Nicky Rossiter, me Da, did not make waves but he sent out ripples over his ninety years that radiated afar and touched people in many ways. From a life spent entirely in his hometown he made many friendships, whether through travelling with the Organisation of Ex-Servicemen and Women to conferences and church parades, by pub outings that started as day trips and evolved into weekends away, or through his penny-farthing bike flowerpot holders that travelled the world.

Today, when we measure people too often by headlines, we forget the foundation of all our lives – the people who make so much happen but seldom get or seek any recognition.

Nicky lived over half of his long life on a single mile or so of a Wexford road, stretching from Pierce's corner to just beyond Browne's corner. His entire working life was spent in Pierce's. He saw the boom times, working overtime and night shifts. He saw the down times of work shortages, takeovers and sit-ins. Not many people know that Mary O'Brien wrote a poem based on part of his working life. It includes the lines:

I'd pass through to the welding shop
where the air was scorched and ozone
my Da a figure in dungarees and mask,
the welding rod a sparkling firework
fizzing in his hand.
A wonder world of work,
They made me welcome there
A man among the men,
Paddy Curran, Hopper and my Da.

Despite the long and hard hours of foundry work, he had a habit of throwing himself heart and soul into all the social activities he got involved in over the years. One of the most outstanding was probably joining the LDF at the age of twenty,

This picture from the 1930s shows an outlying part of the Pierce Works, where they had a sheet-metal fabrication plant. It was on the site of part of the old Bishopswater Distillery and the buildings may have been some of the old stores. The Casa Rio houses were built on this site in the 1940s. (Rossiter Collection)

when war broke out and Ireland experienced the Emergency. Like so many, he joined up and devoted his spare time to becoming prepared to defend his country. Friendships made in those dark days lasted to the end of his life.

In peacetime he became a breeder of canaries as a hobby – sometimes branching into budgies. His passion at one time was producing orange-plumed specimens using special feeds. As well as caring for the birds, he was deeply involved in The Wexford Cage Bird Society. The club organised shows, travelled to exhibit and provided overnight security in the halls during the shows. Another hobby saw him design and paint fire screens with pictures of birds and animals on glass, decorated with coloured silver paper.

In the 1960s he became one of the army of volunteers who through blood, sweat and tears devised, built and then helped to run Fr Sinnott's – officially St Joseph's Boys' Club but never called anything else in our house. That decade is filled with his involvement in the club. There was the ill-fated foundation digging – by shovel and pick – that reached about ten feet before being abandoned to move to a different part of the field. There were the field days, weeks of preparation for days that for him started at dawn and ran to dusk. There were the times reverting to his LDF cooking skills on camp at Duncannon Fort. There was pongo on Sunday afternoons with bottle tops, raffle tickets to be collected on Saturday mornings, and committee meetings and house visits from Fr Harry to discuss more plans or fundraising ideas. If memory serves, Nicky was the second last surviving member of the original Fr Sinnott's group.

Fundraising became his great interest in almost every organisation he joined. He was forever trying to think up new ideas or adapt old ones to bring in the few quid for social clubs he got involved in. Life was filled with nap cards, darts for 'a pair of chickens', spot the ball, win a pint, 'the bonus number', the time of the first goal, silver circles, and sweeps on the National. At one time, he even had a special little machine for sealing the nap cards and Saturday mornings saw him and Katie and anyone available using a hand stamp to put combinations of letters on the cards and then rolling them with the machine, ready for next week's sales. It gave him the greatest of joy over the decades to see clubs thrive on those unsung and gruelling activities, always done behind the scenes.

Sometimes, listening to him, you would fear he was a raving alcoholic as he listed the many pubs he was involved in, but you would be wrong. In the almost sixty years that I have known him I could count on one hand the number of times he was over the limit. People of his generation had little spare cash to spend on drink and whatever amount they did drink, they could hold. For him, the pub was the social club and he probably spent more time talking about raising money than drinking. He would recall the Christmas visit to Harry Stones with the Da (his father) for a few drinks and a singsong with the Rossiter and Clancy wings of the family. His LDF days brought him to Beakey's, later Paddy Gore's and The Pike where he 'had a few' just four days before he passed away. In The Pike, his catch call 'Mind your head Ned' will echo for years to come. Jemmy Browne's, Willie Goodison's, The Keyhole, The Sailing Cot, The Phoenix (or Marty Hayden's), The Fair Do and Purcell's were among the 'gentlemen's clubs' he frequented.

But life also threw him some hard knocks. The hardest was losing Katie all too suddenly and a few miles away from him on 14 August 1988. She was buried on their wedding anniversary, 16 August. He kept her link through Roche's Terrace and the Adoration Nuns – her two regular destinations – and he visited both through rain and shine for years until ill health and the loss of Pat Roberts and Peter Healy broke the chain.

In later years his health failed and, coming back from a serious illness, he needed to move to Ely Hospital. Being Nicky Rossiter, this was an opportunity to forge new friendships, to try to think of new fundraising ideas, and to be himself. His time in Ely was enhanced by visits to Castlebridge Day Care Centre on Wednesdays, where he met many people from Katie's family again and made more new friends. In his mid-eighties he jetted off to Lourdes not once but twice, the second time at twelve hours' notice when a place came up. He could never praise too highly the staff and residents in that penthouse floor of Ely and the fact that they allowed him his 'medicine' each night 'to ward off colds'.

On 8 September 2009, he celebrated his ninetieth birthday. For a few hours he had every person descended from himself and Katie – children, grandchildren and great-grandchildren, all of whom he was immensely proud, along with their families – gathered around him, along with his 'big sister' Kitty (who was ninety-two years old the next day) and her family. The photograph of this gathering was beside his bed and having the picture of him and Kitty in the local newspapers gave him a great boost in those last weeks. So too did the fact that he got an advance copy of 'Nicholas's new book', *The Streets of Wexford*, which he showed off to everyone who visited.

Nicky Rossiter slipped away quietly on 1 October, as usual not making a fuss and 'looking forward to seeing Katie'.

Katie and Nicky Rossiter's wedding day. In those days the celebrations ended in time for the happy couple to catch the train to the honeymoon destination. This particular honeymoon was to the exotic destination of Chapelizod in Dublin to some relatives and would be for just a few days. (Rossiter Collection)

PLAYSCHEME

The Playscheme phenomenon hit Wexford in the early 1980s. I recall that Wolfe Tone Villas was probably one of the earliest estates to have a Playscheme, but they soon spread to any good-sized estate with a population of young children. The Ashfield Belvedere Playscheme began in 1983 and would grow over a number of years as a potent force for building a young community into a solid social entity. The basic idea of the Playscheme was the organisation of a week of activities for children of various ages from a community. The projects often started in newly established communities or in older housing estates where a new wave of young children was emerging.

The Ashfield Belvedere scheme fell into the former of these two categories. Ashfield Drive had been in existence for a few years as a local-authority housing estate in the new Clonard parish. With the opening of Belvedere Grove there was an influx of young families, mostly relatively newly married and with young children. Ashfield had 68 homes and Belvedere would add over 100 more to an area on the outskirts of town with little or no social facilities.

Initially, the Playschemes were usually instigated by social workers who saw the potential in these new communities. The parents were motivated and organised into committees and planning commenced. Like all such projects they needed funding. The committee spent months organising fundraising events, from flag days to visiting local businesses seeking sponsorship for events and making weekly collections among the residents.

Next came the programming. This would show the latent talents and skills that these parents probably never knew they had. In those early months they calculated the number of young people who would need to be entertained in the Playscheme. These were then subdivided into age groups. In the approximately 200 homes there would be about 400 young people of varying ages, interests and abilities to be catered for. Realising the vast number that were to be involved, the committee had to seek outside assistance to help supervise and interact with the young people. Surprisingly there was no shortage of volunteers, as older teenagers from all areas of the town put their names forward as helpers.

During Playscheme Week there needed to be activities to cater for the under fives, the primary school age groups (who were in the majority) and the older teenagers who were probably most in need of activities but could be the most difficult to accommodate.

The week commenced on a Sunday with a parade and in the early years with open-air Mass celebrated in a lorry in one or other of the estates. Local bands and majorettes took part and the afternoon was a sort of street party. From Monday

The 1980s saw a craze for Playschemes sweep the estates of Wexford town. This picture is from the Ashfield Belvedere Playscheme *c.*1983, as volunteers and organisers wait for the parade. The people in the foreground are Anne Furlong, Phil Lyons and Jimmy O'Reilly. (Rossiter Collection)

Pictured at the wall between Clonard church and the Wexford GAA park are the Playscheme children with artist Tony Robinson (right). They are completing a set of superhero murals, featuring characters from comics rather than from the video games that were still decades in the future. (Rossiter Collection)

This is a good-humoured collection of young participants waiting for one of the many Playscheme activities to kick off. (Rossiter Collection)

through to Friday there would be a timetable of events, from open-air arts and crafts with youngsters to football matches, history clue hunts and mural painting for the older children.

Luckily the Playscheme phenomenon coincided with the advent of a community artist project at Wexford Arts Centre, and these individuals, initially Tony Robinson and later Anne Heffernan, would give generously of their professional ability to the children and communities during the week, but also on a longer-term basis.

Every Playscheme had its 'visit to the seaside'. This logistical nightmare was taken on every year and saw fleets of buses ferry the few hundred children and volunteers to Curracloe beach – after weeks of praying that it would be fine. It is only in hindsight that one wonders at the foolhardy optimism that prevailed and helped such expeditions to succeed. Imagine 400 youngsters and about 60 adult and teenage volunteers spread over the dunes and beach and the sense of responsibility felt by the organisers. Thankfully such expeditions proved not only safe but highly successful and popular, and they went off without major incident. For the older teenagers there was an overnight stay at the youth hostel in Rosslare Harbour.

Another popular part of Playscheme was the fire brigade visit. This coincided with the weekly training night of the fire service and would see the red engines descend on the green to extend ladders, demonstrate using hoses and of course give rides in the tenders.

Another fun aspect of Playscheme was the parents versus volunteers football match, when children saw the parents 'let their hair down' to tog out in fancy dress to take on the teenagers in a fun match. The week ended with the Sunday night disco for all involved and organisers vowing 'never again', but already planning how to raise the funds for next year.

The Ashfield Belvedere Playscheme ran for a few years and eventually led to the construction of a community centre at Coolcotts that would give the youngsters of the area a sort of year-round Playscheme, while also offering facilities to senior citizens.

RELIGION

In the early part of the past half-century, religion dominated our lives. It marked each day, week and year, but in many ways our involvement in it was less emphasised than in later decades. We were side-altar participants at weddings, parents might not even attend baptisms and even First Holy Communions might be semi-private affairs.

In the middle years of the twentieth century, baptism was often seen as an urgent need rather than as a family celebration. With infant mortality rates higher than we currently experience, there was seen to be an urgency in having the child christened. If born in hospital, the ceremony might happen there. Otherwise the godparents usually completed the ceremony within a few days of birth. In those days it was not the big family celebration on the altar, but was usually carried out privately at the baptismal font located at the back of the church. There were few people present and there was not the big party to follow. Baptism was seen as a necessity to save the soul from Limbo.

Either the mother missed this ceremony, taking place so soon after the birth, or it was combined with her 'churching'. In Christian tradition the churching of women is the ceremony wherein a blessing is given to mothers after recovery from childbirth. The ceremony includes thanksgiving for the woman's survival of childbirth. It was formerly regarded as unwise for a woman to leave her house to go out at all after confinement until she went to be churched. At one time it is said that mothers who had yet to be churched were regarded as attractive to the fairies, and so in danger of being kidnapped by them.

Most, if not all, education was Church based, with boys and girls usually attending convent schools for the first three years – for junior and senior infants and then first class. The boys usually graduated to the Christian Brothers for second class onwards. In such schools there was an emphasis on religious education in all sorts of ways including the famous or infamous catechism, with its graded questions marked in blue, red and black, as well as the visit by Fr Anglim to test your religious knowledge.

There were also the collections for the 'black babies', usually the domain of an elderly non-teaching nun. There would also be the sale of magazines like the red-covered *Messenger of the Sacred Heart* and *The Far East*, recounting the tales on the missions. These were sent home each month and the money sent back by return. You might even get extra brownie points if you got your granny or auntie to buy a copy.

At home, religion was also apparent. Every home had a Sacred Heart picture with the special red lamp with a crucifix-shaped element burning before it. It is said that those lamps, which replaced the candles, were a major force in the rural electrification of Ireland in the twentieth century. Some psychologists must have marvelled at those pictures, with the image of Christ and His heart exposed, and their effect on vulnerable minds.

The mention of those votive lamps remind me that what we now see advertised as tea lights (wherever that comes from) were night lights in our younger days. They we used as votive lights in front of religious symbols but they also provided illumination for children's rooms through the night. They were usually lit and stood in a saucer of water – early fire prevention – and the burning time of eight hours worked out just right. Another use of the night light was to burn before the May altar which was a feature of most homes in that month. The preparation and maintenance of the May altar was usually the responsibility of the children. Constant queries by the nuns and brothers ensured that the tradition survived.

Feast days loomed large in those days. We had the blessing of throats on 2 February, the feast of St Blaise. This was said to prevent sore throats throughout the year. St Anthony's Day was associated with lillies of the same name. St Patrick's Day was of course the big day, with its parades and Irish entertainment.

In the past, the Old Pound or St Peter's Square was a gathering point for everything from political rallies to religious processions. Here we see Bishop Herlihy leading what is probably a Corpus Christi procession. (Courtesy of Kiernan/Scanlon Collection)

Easter brought the devotions such as Holy Thursday Mass, the Passion on Good Friday, Kissing the Cross on the Friday evening and Midnight Mass on Easter Saturday night. These ceremonies still take place but they all seemed so much longer and more packed a few decades ago.

There were fewer big religious feast days throughout the summer months. As winter drew in, of course, there was November, the month for remembering the dead. This was preceded by the compilation of the Dead List, when families wrote out the lists of deceased relatives to be sent to the priest for inclusion in the Masses of November.

At age seven came the preparation for First Holy Communion. This was a major milestone leading to that first encounter in the confession box, as seven-year-olds tried to conjure up a few sins that, while not soul threatening or likely to bring down the wrath of the priest, were at least bad enough to justify those three Hail Mary's or whatever. There was also the practicing of how to take the host without it touching your teeth and learning to swallow it whole.

This picture recalls the official opening of the Christian Brothers Primary School in Green Street in 1939. Part of the grounds behind the wall was under bushes and trees in the 1960s and a bicycle shed was built to the left. The area has since been built over with classrooms. Note the old-style Garda uniforms.

The Christian Brothers' Band, 1980s. This band was an integral part of the education scene throughout the 1900s. The photograph is taken during a St Patrick's Day parade and shows the ban leading the Clonard section up The Faythe past Barragry's shop. (Rossiter Collection)

After confession came the big day, and in preparation for that came the togging out. In the 1950s the boys still had short pants as part of that first suit for Holy Communion. It was usually a tweed suit, big and chunky with heavy leather shoes and knee socks and possibly a pullover. There was also the white rosette with the medal. The girls were togged out uniformly in white dresses and veils.

Students of the Presentation had their special day in the nuns' chapel in the convent before heading off to visit the relations for the few bob – usually a half-crown in the late 1950s. There was also the obligatory Communion photograph in Denis O'Connor's or some other professional photographer's studio.

Having made your communion you were then required to fulfill all the Christian obligations. There was Mass every Sunday and Holy Day. If you were to receive communion you had to fast from midnight. This made early Masses popular, so as not to die of starvation. Regardless of this, the so-called children's Mass was usually at ten o'clock.

This photo shows some pupils of Wexford CBS Secondary School with two of their teachers, Mr Murphy, who taught bookkeeping, and Mr Byrne, who taught English and Latin.

In order to receive Holy Communion you had to get confession every week. This put a big hole in the Saturday, as the combined ranks of young people trooped into the churches after ten Mass to confess. It was interesting to study the strategies as we tried to guage the speed with which the queues moved, while taking into account the 'tough' priests who might explode at your grave indiscretions. Each confession box had rows of youngsters 'scootching' along, trying to look holy and not to hear the people in the box who expressed their sins a little too loudly.

Your turn came. You knelt in the dark, hearing the muttering from the other side. The grill slammed open and you were off. 'Bless me father for I have sinned; it has been one week since my last confession' and so on at a rate of knots to fly through the chosen sins – half hoping he might miss any biggie, segueing into your Act of Contrition as soon as he passed sentence of Hail Marys, Our Fathers or maybe even a rosary. Out of the box you went towards the altar to serve the penance and then, with a skip in your step, you're off down the aisle and free for another week.

Saturday and Sunday weren't your only church dates though. Wednesday was Confraternity Day and that meant five o'clock in Rowe Street church come hail, shine or any sort of fun games. You could not escape the Confraternity because you were in a section and the prefect of your section had your name and if he did not mark you present the teacher would be making enquiries on Thursday. The Confraternity always seemed to happen on the sunniest evenings – although this has to be selective memory. It was usually about a thirty-minute ceremony starting with the Rosary, followed by a short sermon and then Benediction, with that overpowering smell of incence wafting through the church. It ended, as always, with a spirited rendition

Probably dating from 1932, when the Eucharistic Congress was celebrated, this picture shows the junction of Rowe Street and John Street. The boys have obviously been marching, as they are wearing their sashes.

This picture shows some of the lay participants in the procession at St Peter's Square. Note the children in their First Holy Communion dresses and suits. One of the children appears a bit worse for the wear and is being carried in the left foreground. (Courtesy of Kiernan/Scanlon Collection)

of 'Faith of our Fathers'. In an interesting aside, I found a reference that says that in the early days 'confraternity members were expected to be sober Christians. Those attending wakes, alehouses and idle company could be expelled.'

From First Holy Communion onwards you found another religious obligation looming at regular intervals: the procession. For the uninitiated the procession was a slower and holier version of a parade. The music was provided by the same bands, but the tunes were hymns and they were interspersed with rosaries and other prayers. All of this led to slower movement and thus a longer commitment. The good thing about processions was that they were mostly summer events. Depending on the Church calendar, the first was usually the May procession. This took place on a Monday evening in May from Bride Street church to the Marian Shrine at Rocklands. The locals decorated windows and doorways with altars to Our Lady and flags and bunting decked the streets with larger altars erected at roadsides. The Corpus Christi procession was held on Thursdays, when the shops used to close for the half day, but this later moved to Sunday afternoons. It usually wound its way through the town streets, starting in one of the twin churches to conclude in the other, or in St Peter's Square. In later years they rerouted this and some other processions through the newer estates.

In the 1950s, there were smaller processions for schoolchildren that were held in the grounds of the twin churches. That was before the motor car and before the car park completely overran the grounds. I recall Bride Street chapelyard in particular with a lot more trees and grass and with pathways through the trees that offered lovely procession routes.

Once a year, during Lent, there was a more intense display of religion when the Mission came to town. This was usually spread over three weeks, with one week for children, one for women and one for men. The missioners were visiting priests who had often seen service in foreign lands. There was generally a mix of nice men, and fire and brimstone preachers. The children would be treated to nice tales of derring do and adventures in religion. The ladies probably got similar but more grown-up fare. The men, in their best suits and smelling of hair oil and soap, could be almost guaranteed a verbal roasting to prepare them for hellfire. Part of the Mission also included home visits by the missioners. This meant scrubbed houses, best linen and children on their best behaviour.

The next step in religion was to become a 'soldier of Christ' at Confirmation at the age of twelve, before moving on from primary school. The preparation this time was academic, with your religious knowledge pumped to new heights and an outside examiner – maybe even the bishop – coming to give you the test. Having passed the test it was suit time again. Some parents still insisted that short trousers were okay for twelve year olds and thus there could be major embarrassment with this rite. The photographs still exist to haunt you. Confirmation was administered by the bishop and included the 'slap on the cheek', which we all anticipated as much more than it actually amounted to. We also had to adopt an extra name for Confirmation. The teachers wanted to be sure there was a saint to back up whatever you chose, so there were few film star influences.

Having made your Confirmation you moved on to secondary school, the 'Tech' (as the vocational school was called) or out to work. In secondary school we met another religious practice, the Retreat. This was a bit like the Mission but it was 'in house'. For about a week, classes were suspended and we spent the days in prayer and quiet meditation. We drifted from room to room with religious tracts looking oh so holy, or sat in contemplation of life. It was really a bit of a doss but it could also make time drag. The Retreat was a time when vocations were invoked and visting religious men told us of the attractions of their lives.

During the secondary-school years were were also encouraged to join religious groups like the St Vincent de Paul Society or the Legion of Mary. These were potentially very interesting groups, but we became swamped with the praying side and most people drifted away. I recall the Legion of Mary book and meetings in a room in the monastery, but I do not recall too many of them so I must have drifted rather rapidly.

The St Vincent de Paul building in Francis Street. (Courtesy of Kiernan/Scanlon Collection)

For those not in receipt of a vocation to the religious life, the next event where religion impinged was marriage. By the 1970s this had expanded to include compulsory instruction and the ceremony was a major part of the wedding Mass but I recall attending weddings where it was far from being quite so centre stage.

In the 1950s and 1960s, weddings usually took place on the side altar before a seven o'clock Mass in the morning, giving the true meaning to that wedding meal as a 'wedding breakfast'. There was little pomp and ceremony with organs, singers, confetti and speeches, unless it was for one of the gentry.

One interesting aspect of marriage at the time was the banns. These were the three consecutive weekly announcements at Sunday Mass of the names and addresses of those intending to marry and the call for any objections involving 'consanguinity, affinity or any other sort' to be made known as soon as possible. I wonder how many times objections derailed romances.

The final religious rite was of course the funeral. Again, in those times the funeral was less obvious. There were no eulogies or gifts brought up. The priest usually gave a generic sermon and music or singing was for special people. The one thing that funerals did evoke was the genuine sympathy and show of support from friends, neighbours and townspeople. People took time off work to walk after a funeral, much more so than today. Shops closed their doors as the cortège passed – from Bride Street they used go down Bride Street, South Main Street and King Street to the quay. I recall the train stopping on the quay as my Granda Walsh's funeral passed, but that may have been because he worked for CIE.

Above left: In the 1970s, priestly duties could easily include all manner of fundraising. Here we find Fr Dan Nolan of Clonard, with parishioners Joe Brennan and Nicky Kehoe, manning a stand at the Bullring selling tickets for a raffle to win a mustard-coloured car with black top. (Courtesy of Kiernan/Scanlon Collection)

Above right: The Friends Meeting House was at Patrick's Square in 1842. According to Bassett, in 1885 the caretaker was Jane Jones. The hall became home to the Loch Garman Silver Band and was a popular venue for bird shows in the 1950s. (Rossiter Collection)

The Sisters of Mercy Nuns were established on 8 December 1840 at Paul Quay and later moved to Clarence House in High Street. They took over the Redmond Talbot Orphanage at Summerhill in 1842 and there they established a House of Mercy in 1865 to train girls as servants. St Michael's Industrial School for Roman Catholic Girls was certified in 1869. In 1902, St Michael's was classed as one of top three schools for training girls for domestic service. (Rossiter Collection)

In the homes of the deceased, blinds were drawn for the duration, from death to burial. A black crepe adorned the door. Televisions and radios were silent until after the burial and close family wore black for a long period afterwards. The 'black diamond' sewn onto a sleeve became popular in place of the mourning band with the material shortage during the Emergency. The 'ninth day' was a solemn ceremony when those who might not have been able to attend the burial gathered at the cemetery for prayers and possibly return to the house for refreshments.

There were even specific rates offered by hackney cars for such events, and in 1968 the set rates from Bride Street to Crosstown were £1 10s and Rowe Street to Crosstown £1 5s. The ninth day car rate was 15s. Wedding cars cost £1 10s, and for a christening, the car would set you back 12s 6d.

The Month's Mind and anniversary Masses, advertised in the local newspapers, were observed for years afterwards.

ST JOSEPH'S REVISITED

We looked at the history of St Joseph's Boys' Club (or Fr Sinnott's as it was more widely known) in an earlier book, but as other material comes to light we revisit this unusual institution with some interesting snippets.

The official opening concert took place on Sunday 14 October 1962. Among those cajoled – probably by Fr Harry – to take paid advertising space in the programme were the usual retail outlets, but also some unusual ones. These included the FCA seeking recruits, shops like the Gem and Tommy Curtis's in far away George's Street and Michael Street respectively, and one that was from Nicholas Swords, Monck Street that said nothing about a business or telephone contact – was he that well known?

Bishop Staunton in his written address apologised for missing the event. The opening extravaganza was performed by St Brigid's Concert Group and was staged on two nights. Among the performers were:

Sweets of May – Irish Figure Dance
Songs by Nancy Doyle, soprano
Step Dancing by P. Kehoe & P. O'Reilly
Pick of the Pops from Eddie Hopkins's Showband
Songs by Seamus Cullen, tenor
Selection of Airs by Slaneyside Céilí Band
'Kevin Barry' listed as a dramatised song
Violin Solo – Sean Rattigan

St. Joseph's Boys' Club
will guide you to manhood.

You can repay the debt by giving a term of your manhood to your country's colours.

Do so with the Wexford

F. C. A.

Particulars of enlistment at military Bks., Wexford
Monday nights from 7.30

This is one of the more interesting advertisements featured in the programme book for the opening of St Joseph's Club. (Rossiter Collection)

Alvina Brook was built shortly after 1940 by Pierces. Numbers 3 and 4 were used for Corporation lettings. There were no numbers 1 and 2. (Rossiter Collection)

Irish Step Dancing – The Hopkins Sisters

Songs by Peter Murphy

A medley of Irish Dancing by The Gaul School

There was also a one-act operetta

The first sod had been dug on Monday 5 September 1960, the same night the Wexford hurlers returned after defeating Tipperary in the All-Ireland. As bonfires blazed and crowds greeted the hurling heroes, the unsung heroes of St Joseph's toiled until dusk fell.

Although two years elapsed from sod to opening, the club was actually built in about eighty weeks. Work was suspended during the winter months of December to April each year. It was estimated that the average number of hours devoted to construction by those volunteers was forty-five per week. This was an amazing commitment when we consider that most if not all worked similar hours each week at full-time, often gruelling work.

The club was designed by John Hendrick of Alvina Brook and work was carried out under his supervision. The site was land made available by John Conboy of Rathaspeck. Dr Frank Keenan consented to be the club doctor and H.B. Brandon Ferguson Chartered Accountants looked after the books, with Tom Keeling advising the club. The materials were purchased locally from Wexford Timber Company, McCormack Brothers, Wilsonite Concrete Products and O'Rourke Brothers. Club nights were Sunday 7.30p.m. to 10p.m. and Monday, Wednesday and Thursday, 7.00p.m. to 9.30p.m.

THE GRAND ANNUAL COLLECTION

It may be hard to believe, but a little over a century ago your donation to the church was far from anonymous. In those years, the donors towards the upkeep of the parish churches known as the Grand Annual Collection were published – with amounts of their donations – in the local newspapers. A quick look over the list is most interesting and informative for the local historian, as it reminds one of the people of the town and the addresses of that period.

To take 1943 in the midst of war as an example, we find that Bishop Staunton was the prime donor, with ten guineas. This was matched by John Healy of Alma, while a tenner came from Patrick Kelly of Cornmarket. Other donors above £5 included: People Newspapers; James Corry, Peace Commissioner, Rowe Street; P.J. Clarke of the National Bank; Dr McCabe in Selskar; Laurence Kirwan, solicitor, Lorneville; James Whelan, Moongate; the Misses Harpur of Waterloo Road; Andrew Nolan of Fortview; Loch Garman Co-op; Francis Rochford, Westgate; Patrick Meyler, John Street; Harry Wilson, Slaney House; P.V. McSwiney, Munster & Leinster Bank, and separate donations from J.J. Stafford of Cromwell's Fort personally and from his companies such as Wexford Timber Company, Wexford Steamship Company and J.J. Stafford & Sons. The piece then lists £5 donations from such people and institutions as Fintan M. O'Connor, Westlands, Dr Daly MOH, Wm Corcoran of *The Free Press*, Laurence Kirwan, Ballinagee and Wexford Gas Company.

Other interesting randomly selected entries include J.J. Stafford Jr at Cromwell's Fort giving £3, the same sum donated by the Misses O'Keefe in The Faythe. The Christian Brothers, the Cinema Palace, John Kearney of Selskar, Mr McGovern, inspector of taxes, and P.G. Lambert the auctioneer each put up two guineas.

In the £1 donations we find Chief Superintendent Mooney of the Garda Síochána; Captain Murphy, St John's Road; Gordon & Furlong, plumbers; Phil Kenny, Imperial Hotel; Captain Hearne, Arran Cottage; Nurse Gaul of Carrigeen, and Captain Delaney of Parnell Street. Other intriguing entries include 'Nano and Nello', A Friend, Mrs Neady, a number of individual gardaí, and Patrick Keating (RAF) Cornmarket.

In total, just over £1,192 was donated in that year.

THE RAILWAY

Today we do most of our travel by private car and when we do use public transport, despite all our talk of green credentials and global warming, we're more likely to take a bus than a train.

Things were very different in the middle of the twentieth century. For a start, there were more destinations available by train from Wexford, including New Ross. The train was popular for going to GAA matches there. There were also many more stops at small stations along all routes – in the time before speed and express travel elbowed out convenience and community. Who can recall the announcements for stops like Macmine Junction?

In the 1950s, a trip by train was still an adventure, like air travel would become later. Going to Dublin was a big deal, with school educational trips which might include a visit to the zoo (or the 'a-zoo' as many people pronounced it), dinner (as we called the current lunch) in Woolworth's in Henry Street, and maybe a visit to a museum. Such trips were the culmination of the school year and were only available to sixth class, whereas today every class from kindergarten up seem to have a school trip.

The 1950s saw such trips still going under steam power on occasion, with the ever-present danger of 'getting smuts in your eye' if you lowered the window on its leather strap and poked your head out. Those windows were only at the ends of carriages. Thinking back, even the carriages had more character then. There were first, second and even third class carriages at one time and the collector made sure you stayed in your class. We also had the carriages with compartments. These had a passage along the side with a sliding door giving access to each double-facing seated compartment, where one was cut off from the masses tramping up and down corridors.

Permanent lights were not common, so a trip through a tunnel such as the one at Ferrycarrig meant being plunged into darkness, with screams from the novice travellers.

The railway was also the primary carrier of freight in the mid-twentieth century, especially following the closure of the harbour to coastal shipping due to the sandbar. The goods yard at the North Station was a hive of activity, with all manner of goods arriving for immediate delivery or to be warehoused in the sheds there. Companies like Irish Cement had permanent storage facilities there, as did Lyons Tea, whose shed, painted in the colour of its famous green label tea, is still just about standing in the precinct of the station.

Goods arriving by train were transported to factories and shops by horse and cart right into the 1960s. The long cart pulled by the big dray horses was a common sight on the streets of Wexford with Mr Breen at the reins.

Above: On 12 December 1872, a dinner celebrated the start of work on the Wexford–Waterford line. In the 1950s it was common for hundreds of people to crowd Wexford stations to see off people heading to England for work or returning to work after a holiday home. Tickets costing 1*d* each were needed to access the platform. (Rossiter Collection)

Left: Close-up showing the exquisite detail that went into railway stations in the boom years of that form of transport. (Rossiter Collection)

Here we see Trinity Street, the signal box and derelict platform of the South Station, Chadwick's and the gasometers from the unusual angle of the seaward side. (Rossiter Collection)

This picture dating from the removal of the Woodenworks, gives us a chance to see the Belvedere that once adorned the custom house on the corner of the Crescent. It also shows the old Stafford Coal buildings along Paul Quay and the gasometers. (Rossiter Collection)

With so much freight arriving and departing, goods trains were a common sight on the quays, as they had been in earlier decades when used to load and unload cargoes from the boats at the quay. These made the quay front a much busier location than it is today and when we consider that it was much narrower with boats, two rail tracks and the road all within about thirty yards, we get an idea of a different town. Try to imagine a passenger train on the solid surface passing a goods train full of machinery or chocolate crumb parked on the Woodenworks with a boat unloading timber on to the quayside, as cars and lorries passed by on the road. Add to this people strolling along the Woodenworks and young chancers putting pennies on the tracks to be flattened by the train and you have to wonder how there were not more numerous accidents. The only fatal accident I can recall was that of Mr Pierce from S&R Pierce, who died when a train struck his car as he exited the goods yard one afternoon.

The opening of the New Bridge in 1959 added to the potential for incidents between trains and cars, in that it gave us an unmanned crossing at the junction policed only by flashing lights and a clanging bell. The older bridge at Carcur had seen the trains pass under a road bridge. At the South Station, those working in or visiting the factories like Clover Meats, Smiths or the Star crossed the tracks. Further south, the people accessing Browne's Bank or the Cott Safe would cross the tracks as others did further along the south slob lands.

This picture reminds us of older days in Wexford when seafaring was in the blood and many families maintained small boats for fishing or leisure and moored them at the Cott Safe below Batt Street. The trawler is passing the site where once stood industries like Clover Meats, The Star Engineering Works, Smiths Assembly Plant and Wexford Electronix. (Rossiter Collection)

Today the scheduled trains are few, and are set to be fewer, so before they are gone completely you should take the train to Rosslare and see a view of our county that will be witnessed by fewer people with each passing year.

Above: Here we see the old South Station in all its glory, with two tracks and a double platform. The track runs past where the old Steam Packet Wharf stood, taking passengers by sea from Wexford to Tenby and other destinations. (Rossiter Collection)

Left: On a reclaimed site jutting out into the harbour at the south end of Wexford was The Star Iron Works. It was also the site of Clover Meats at one time. (Rossiter Collection)

THE SEVENTIES

They say that if you remember the Sixties you weren't there, and in many ways the Eighties are best forgotten, so I decided to look at some of the local happenings of the Seventies to help to jog a few memories.

A maximum price order was put on drink in Wexford in 1973. This reminds me of the names of the publicans in business in Wexford at the time. We had Tommy Beaky in Barrack Street, where we now have The Pike. I remember that his son John was in my class in the secondary school. Joe Lambert was in the Bullring before the premises became a boutique. Jimmy Browne of Bishopswater, my first employer, also owned The Tower Bar at the time and Paddy Purcell had his premises in The Faythe. An interesting point showing the power and influence of trade unions of the day is that the Trades Council had been instrumental in the minister bringing in the order.

Down in Kilmore the local newspapers reported that Johnny Sinnott had a lucky escape when his car went over the quay. Luckily it caught on a rope securing a trawler and was pulled out with the help of a tractor.

In Rosslare Harbour, CIE was seeking planning permission for an open-air swimming pool, squash and tennis courts at the Great Southern Hotel.

Miss Mary Dunphy, who was on holidays in Furziestown, Tacumshane, from her home in California, found a message in a bottle at Rostoonstown. Sadly it was not from an exotic desert island but rather from someone in Bishopstown in Cork.

In Enniscorthy, Michael Smith of Drumgoold Villas retired after serving fourteen years with Sisk & Co. He got a presentation of a wallet of notes which appears to have been the approved retirement present – more useful than a travel or carriage clock, or the gold watch that seemed to feature in so many fictional retirements.

Patrick Power and Dick Hayes Junior travelled to Hull to study echo sounders, indicating the arrival of new technology in the fishing industry.

John Murphy's 166-acre farm at Ballingale Taghmon was sold for £60,000.00. Meanwhile, a bungalow at Mulgannon in Wexford fetched £12,000.00.

Pat Quinn – famous for his bald head and white polo neck sweaters (a fashion of the era) – was the new owner of The Castle Motor Hotel back in 1973. This is now Hotel Ferrycarrig. Pat paid a visit to the hotel by helicopter at a time when such occurrences were reported in the papers. He landed in the GAA park.

In the summer of 1973, we were eagerly awaiting the opening of our swimming pool, sunbathing area, restaurant and soft drinks bar at Ferrybank. This was built on the romantic Dairy Fields.

The Regal Lodge Roadhouse out the Newline or Duncannon Road was a very popular entertainment venue at the time. The acts on offer ranged from the local band Kinsella Country to Brendan Grace. You got both on a single bill with the Kinsella billing bigger than the comedian.

The Castlebridge Hotrod Club was presenting racing at Kilrane. Admission was 20p. There was also a children's sports programme on offer. It was noted that Fintan Murphy gave use of the field.

Wexford Rifle Club was presenting a film show at the Dun Mhuire. The double bill included *The Art of Small Bore Shooting* and a nature film called *Oisin*. Admission was free.

In Broadway there was a charity walk led by St Patrick's Fife & Drum Band and there was a dance the same night with Bob Ormsby and his band. Both were in aid of the Old Folks' Party.

A Ford Anglia dominates the right-hand corner of this picture of Redmond Square. These were very popular cars in the 1970s. The bus behind the Redmond Monument is a CIE vehicle probably bound for Dublin from the North Station. (Courtesy of Kiernan/Scanlon Collection)

You may have noted that a number of these attractions were outside the urban area and that 1973 would not have been an era of many cars. The organisers got over this potential difficulty by bussing in the patrons. For a dance in Rosslare Harbour the bus could collect dance enthusiasts from Castlebridge, Murrintown, Kilmore Cross Roads, Tenacre Cross and Bridgetown. There were pick-up times printed in the advertisements.

Tommy Carroll was popular in those days, with two gigs in one week, although his cordovox appears to have been billed only once. The Menapia Folk remind us that the ballad boom had not died in rural Wexford.

Taking the car, bus or bike into town opened up a world of variety in the Dun Mhuire. Top of the bill were The Pattersons – another folk outfit. Joe Lynch was billed as coming directly from a TV station but not *Glenroe*. At the time he was starring with David Kossoff in *Never Mind the Quality – Feel the Width* on ITV.

George Boyle was popular on what we then knew as Telefís Éireann, with a show called *Seorsa agus Beartlaí*. I wonder whatever happened to Rose Cousins, billed as the 'showbiz find of '71'?

For the younger dancers, disco had arrived, with go-go dancers, light shows and 'films – with sound'. Admission was only ten bob and you got chicken and chips thrown in.

For a more sedate and probably romantic night out, how could you pass up Castlebridge Ballroom for 8s, with dancing from 9 to 1? You also had the chance to see the three Kinsella brothers as part of The Blue Mountain Boys.

Do you remember the height of fashion in those days for the lads? Yes those were the days of 'car coats'. Remember them? Short jackets with fake fur on the collar. The older generation described them precisely as 'bum freezers' in the days when we all had the coats but few, if any, had the car.

THE WAY WE SPOKE

Like many towns or even countries, we often assume that words or expressions are unique to us. It is only when researched we usually discover that these words have crept in from other cultures or continents. But this does not disqualify them. There are few unique expressions anywhere in the world; even Cockney rhyming slang and the English language itself borrow things from others.

One anomaly I have noticed over the years is the way different countries' residents refer to mothers. In America she is usually Mom or Mommy, in Britain this changes to Mum or Mummy, and in Ireland in general it is Mammy or, less often, Mam. In Wexford the most common cry is 'me Ma'.

Showing two aspects of old Wexford, we have the man driving a horse and cart with what appears to be scrap, and a woman wheeling a child in a tansad at the top of George Street. (Courtesy of Kiernan/ Scanlon Collection)

This is a reminder of times long past, in the mode of transport and the ability to stop and chat on John's Street. The short trousers and knobbly knees on the youngsters provide some nostalgia. (Courtesy of Kiernan/Scanlon Collection)

Although not all our expressions are unique, I have to admit that many of them can sound pretty much Wexford regardless of where they started and they will always remind people of this town when heard at home or a thousand miles away.

For instance, Rossiter is usually pronounced as 'Roster' by the true older generation of Wexfordian. Jim O'Neill would be 'Jem Nail' and James Browne's pub was 'Jemmy Browne's'.

Two words that I associate with home shoe repairing, but that I cannot find in standard dictionaries, are 'sparbles' and 'heel ball'. Sparbles was the name for the little nails used for tacking on the leather sole or heel. Heel ball was a block of colouring that may have been wax. It gave the colouring for the edge of the leather used for 'soling and heeling' the shoes, to blend with the shoe colour. Heel ball also occurred in an expression relating to appearance or attitude, in the phrase 'He was all heel ball', meaning a person looking well spruced up for a date.

Ants were often referred to as 'Pismires', which turns out to be a proper name for a species of ant, with the first part coming from Middle English for urine, based on the smell of the acid they secrete, and myre from Danish for ant. Here we see an example of those non-local Wexford words.

We used 'perish' in both its meanings quite commonly into recent times, although it has fallen out of general usage. One phrase of course was 'perishing with the cold', which was quite an eloquent use of the word, but another great epithet was when you vexed someone and they would say, 'that will be the rock you will perish on'. Looking at that sentence I wonder how many people use the word 'vexed'.

To orient the viewer here, the sign for Kearney's Funeral Furnishers is at the corner of Slaney Street. The company is currently located further along Selskar Street. The yard full of builder's rubbish is now occupied by Dunnes Stores. (Courtesy of Kiernan/Scanlon Collection)

Looking north from Coffin Corner we see Andy Kinsella's pub on our right then Malone's fish shop, and across Oyster Lane is Londis Pettit's food market, where the family business started with Jackie. (Courtesy of Kiernan/Scanlon Collection)

Closely related to perishing in the former phrase is a lovely expression for being very cold. My mother often said, 'We were spar blasted waiting for the bus.' This meant extremely cold and probably has nautical origins (as in relating to the spar on a ship).

Another Wexford phrase that is unique to the town but probably has counterparts in every other town in the world is to say, 'He must have been made in Pierce's.' This was a comment used when a person showed little or no emotion, indicating a non-human origin. I suppose Pierce's is replaced by a myriad of factories worldwide, but this particular phrase is ours.

Crepe was used most commonly for a crumpled tissue paper, usually in various colours, long before it was common parlance for pancakes. The paper usually made its most common appearance at Christmas to cover the bucket holding the Christmas tree, to wrap presents or to make decorations. A characteristic of crepe paper was that it was sort of elastic and this gave rise to another expression that can seem a bit rude today but it was very common in the late 1900s. If an item shrunk in the wash, one might say it 'crapped', meaning it went like crepe paper. The word also had a more sombre meaning in that it referred to the bow, often of black net-type material, that was fixed to the front door of a deceased person's home, with a card attaching giving funeral arrangements.

We might sometimes have used words that were common in English but we might have modified their meaning. In general, 'wainscoting' is said to refer to the wood panelling used to cover the lower half of the walls of a room – most commonly an entrance hall. In Wexford, the name was often applied to what is commonly called the skirting board.

If you use the internet to look up the word 'sprong', what Wexford people for years have called the garden fork, be prepared for a surprise. It is given many definitions, from 'a five-character sequence of C-code' to 'strands of hair that remain in place after combing' to a naughty one.

Coincidentally, we refer to that hair condition as a 'cow's lick', but I find we are not exclusive in this.

Another phrase I always associate with me Ma is, 'I was parchin' with the droot.' This was parching with the drought and as you will agree it was a very descriptive way of saying you were thirsty, by bringing visions of parched lands and an actual drought. The remedy could be a 'bottle of minerals', or as the British might say a 'bottle of pop', indicating a soft drink. Katie's ideal remedy was a glass of Cousins Orange Crush, a large bottle of which was always on hand. Here she was supporting her former employer and local industry.

Speaking of minerals reminds me of that sweet that we called a 'kayli'. It was a sherbert that came sometimes in a bag with a lollypop and at other times it was in a sort of tube – like a stick of dynamite – with a liquorice straw. Once again the myth explodes as we find it was not a Wexford exclusive.

Adults, of course, were past masters of language. Nowhere is this more evident than with the word 'feck'. Any adult could, and did, use this word, with its various adaptations, without 'fear or favour' when everyone knew they really meant a similar work with an alternative vowel. Mind you, the word was also used as an alternative to steal, as in, 'Did you feck that book?' It was also useful as 'leave', in the sense that 'He fecked off home.' It is said to have also been used as a substitute for 'throw', but I have not experienced this in Wexford. Further investigation finds the word in literature of Robert Louis Stevenson and in song by Robbie Burns, with even more meanings.

For some reason we also often pronounced loan as 'loand'. So, while our words may not be completely our own invention, we certainly took possession of them and used them to great effect.

COURT CASES

Crime and court cases are still a great source of distraction in the media. In this section we look at a selection of interesting or unusual cases that were publicly reported in Wexford in the past. In the interest of fairness we will refrain from using the names of those involved.

BREAKING AND ENTERING

In 1945, William was brought before Eamon O'Riain, acting District Justice, charged with breaking and entering a dwelling house in Mary's Lane. He is said to have stolen a gramophone sound box valued at 2s 6d, two girls' skirts valued 27s and one pair of Wellington rubber boots valued 18s. Another person was charged with receiving the boots.

Mr Godfrey appeared as solicitor for both defendants. The latter admitted receiving the boots but claimed he did not know they were stolen. The house in question was that of a general dealer and he was accustomed to locking it up and being away for up to a month at a time. On returning he found the house had been entered by removing a window.

It transpired that the defendant had sold the boots to the dealer for 10s earlier. In defence, Godfrey said the window had been open and the defendant had no money because he was out of work. His father was said to be in hospital in England and unable to support the family. He pleaded that poverty was the reason for the theft if not the excuse.

It turned out that although only aged twenty years, his criminal career had started five years before and he had been given the Probation Act, spent time in Glencree and been imprisoned for six months prior to this charge. He got another prison sentence.

TURF THEFT

In 1939, two women were charged with stealing a quantity of turf, the property of Fuel Importers Ltd at the South Railway Station. The superintendent gave evidence that 'one of the defendants went with her husband's dinner, accompanied by the other defendant'. He said they had two sacks with them and were discovered returning with a quantity of turf. The turf was eventually recovered.

BATON CHARGE

'Mister D.' was charged with disorderly behaviour in 1939. The prosecuting guard reported that when refused drink, the defendant 'hit the publican a blow with his fist in the stomach'. He then kicked the witness and came to strike him. The guard used his baton in self-defence.

Mr Louth, solicitor for the defendant, said his client had 'rather too much drink taken'. He said he had gone through the First World War and was discharged with malaria and shellshock. With the guard forced to use his baton the defendant was out of work for a fortnight and it was felt that this was punishment enough. The justice fined him £2.

Above left: Oak's Lane runs parallel to Charlotte Street, one shop width to the south. It is now in a sad state, being used as a storage area and worse. It is worth the effort to follow the lane from North Main Street to the quay. This lane was referred to as the Old Shambles in a map of the 1840s. (Rossiter Collection)

Above right: Paul Quay was variously said to take its name from Paul Turner (a landowner), 'pale', meaning a fortress, or 'pole', meaning a river. The pale could refer to the castle or barracks which once dominated the area. The pole could be the Horse River, which enters the harbour at the small bridge here. The Mercy Nuns started here, and it was later a technical school, a hat factory, the Masonic Order HQ and the Penny Dinners. (Rossiter Collection)

ADMISSION TO AN INDUSTRIAL SCHOOL

In 1880, Mary Farrell applied to have a child, her stepdaughter, admitted to St Michael's Industrial School. The child was eleven years of age and was destitute, her mother being dead eleven years and her father dying about five months earlier.

Sir F. Hughes asked, 'Have you not the same means to support her now that you had for the last five months?'

'No, sir, I had a trifle when her father died, but it is gone, and I have not what will support myself now.'

Mr Flood believed it was doubtful if the stepmother was not compelled to support her stepchild. The clerk said in the Industrial School Act it was not defined as it only said stepparents and others. The application was granted.

THE WORKHOUSE

In researching this book I found a verbatim report in *The People* newspaper of 21 January 1880. It shows not only the sad circumstances of those admitted to the workhouse but also the commitment that the members of bodies like the Local Government Board or the Board of Guardians brought to what were often unpaid posts. It also demonstrates once again the reporting of highly personal details:

Captain Hamilton, Inspector under the Local Government Board, held an enquiry in the Board-room of the Wexford Workhouse, arising out of the admission of an illegitimate child, whose mother, Mary Murphy, formerly an inmate of the workhouse, died on 14 December. The investigation commenced immediately after the conclusion of the ordinary business of the board. Several of the guardians remained.

Sarah Murphy: I am daughter of the late Mary Murphy. I am nearly sixteen years of age, and I am in the Industrial School. I was formerly in the Workhouse.

Johanna Sutton brought a letter to me, with money in it from Mr Kavanagh. It was not a letter, it was only an envelope. This was about a month before my mother died. I was then in Barrack Street, my mother was living in Castle Street [presumably Castle Hill Street located just above Barrack Street]. I gave her the letter. It contained £1. I asked her where the letter was, and she said no matter. I never saw money received on any other occasion from anybody. I am perfectly certain that Sutton told me the envelope containing the money came from Mr Kavanagh. I met her in the Main Street. My mother sent me to meet her. She told me to go and meet Johanna Sutton, and see it she had a letter for her. I did not know of my mother having any more money. I never heard my mother speaking of Mr Kavanagh, or mention his name.

To Mr Kavanagh: I did not write a letter from my mother to you, asking you to get me a situation.

Mr Kavanagh: I received such a letter and I thought it was your handwriting.

Mr Cooney: Did you speak to anyone about the evidence you should give here to-day? – I spoke to Mrs Irwin, the schoolmistress. I met her in Wexford before I got the letter. I got the letter about a week after meeting her. She asked me if I liked the place I was in and I said no, and she said she would have me taken out of it. I told her I was going for a letter. My mother sent me twice for the letter. I told Mrs Irwin I was going for a letter that Mr Kavanagh was to send my mother, by Johanna Sutton.

Mr Cooney: Did anyone go to the school to tell you what to say here? – No.

Mr Cooney: I see you hesitate; tell the truth, you are in a very awkward position?

Mr N. Codd: Don't frighten the child.

Captain Hamilton: Did anyone call to you to the school?

Sarah Murphy: Mrs Irwin came to the convent and told me I would be brought here, but that was all.

Mr Codd: Did anyone else speak to you about the kind of evidence you should give?

Sarah Murphy: No

Mr Irwin: Did Mrs Hore call to you at the convent?

Sarah Murphy: No.

Mr Codd: Were you out on leave?

Sarah Murphy: Yes.

Mr Codd: Were you at Mrs Hore's?

Sarah Murphy: Yes. She told me not to say anything.

Johanna Sutton: I am employed to bring milk to the house from Pembrokestown. On one occasion I brought a letter from Mr Kavanagh, and gave it to Sarah Murphy. Previously she came to me, and asked me if I had a letter for her, from Mr Kavanagh. I did not see him at the time, but one or two days afterwards I asked him, and he answered me very cross, 'No'. A few days afterwards I met him, and he told me he had a letter for Murphy, and would I have any way of giving it to her. I said not, unless I'd see her little girl Sarah. He gave me the letter, and I delivered it to the little girl that evening. Mrs Murphy, herself, gave me a bit of a note for Mr Kavanagh and he wrote on a slip of paper an answer which I gave to her. I never took any other letter. I have occasionally brought Mrs Murphy a grain of tea, and sugar, while she was in this house. This was not with the porter's knowledge. I never asked her where she got the money. She would give me a few pence to buy them. I never saw more than about four pence with her. I never brought her whiskey or porter. Mrs Murphy told me that the note to Mr Kavanagh was asking him about her little girl going to Mrs Sheill. I did not know there was money in the letter I gave the little girl. I never saw much money with her.

Edward Kearns: In reference to the preliminary examination on the 3rd instant in reply to a question put to me by Mr Peacocke whether I ever saw any flush of money with the deceased, in the confusion and excitement of the moment I said I had no recollection of having seen money with her, but I recollect that in the month of October I remarked to the matron that I had seen plenty of money with her, that she had more money than I had considering our relative positions.

Captain Hamilton: Here is your evidence before the committee, 'Mary Murphy was my servant in the lodge. I never saw or knew any immorality going on, nor did I suspect any. She was in the performance of her duty frequently in the Boardroom. I never suspected she was in the family-way. I never noticed money with her.'

E. Kearns: Yes, and I want to correct the last statement about the money. I was appointed the first week in March during my father's illness and Mary Murphy was appointed my servant. She was to clean down the boardroom and the clerk's office, I remarked she would come up when the clerk would be here, but it never occurred to me that there was anything improper between them. I never heard of her being in the family way till the 18th. I said to you that Mrs Murphy exhibited a very free manner towards Mr Kavanagh, was impertinent and went up to the boardroom hot foot after him. She would be sometimes half an hour in the boardroom and I never noticed anything in her appearance after coming down. She did not in my opinion remain longer than necessary.

This picture of Maudlintown brings us back to the days of Denny Murray delivering milk by horse and cart. He had the milk – one variety fits all – in a big can and he doled it out in a long-handled jug into whatever utensil the housewife had to hand. Then there was the so-called 'tilly for the cat', even if you didn't have a feline companion. (Courtesy of Kiernan/Scanlon Collection)

Mr Peacocke: That does not seem to accord with your former evidence.

E. Kearns: She would go up to the kitchen, to the lodge, and about the land. I never knew her to be out by herself or after dark. In my opinion the woman did not remain longer in the boardroom than was necessary. The Clerk spoke to me about my evidence and the master also since the preliminary examination. The clerk said I had compromised him by remarking how long the woman remained in the boardroom, and the master said I had given very unsatisfactory evidence, and ought to clear the character of the house that I had given evasive answers.

Mr Irwin: I should wish to ask the witness while he is on oath if he considers it was through a hostile feeling to the clerk that I made my report.

Captain Hamilton: It is not necessary and he can only be examined on points which affect the case.

Molly Mythen's pub was officially the Thomas Moore Tavern in memory of the national bard whose mother hailed from there. The building had a history much older than Moore, indeed the Ark Club was located there in 1830. (Rossiter Collection)

Mr Irwin: He could give a satisfactory answer to the question, for he knows all about it. Captain Hamilton: Nobody charges you with improper motives, and it was your duty to make the report. I shall now read your evidence at the preliminary inquiry. It is as follows, 'Mr Irwin: Mary Murphy was an inmate for nine years. I knew her from her childhood. Her husband went to America. She became the mother of an illegitimate child. She filled different departments satisfactorily, and was sent to the lodge as a fit person. Among her duties was the lighting of the boardroom fire and cleansing the rooms. An assistant clerk, Mr Gifford, was frequently alone in the boardroom. The clerk was, of course, constantly in the room. I never saw anything wrong going on with any officer. She asked me to let her come before the board for clothes to go to Waterford. I advised her not to go. She persisted. Her daughter, about fourteen, was an attendant in my room. She finally took her discharge. The matron said to me, 'I hope there is nothing wrong with Mrs Murphy.' I spoke to the latter in consequence, and thought there was nothing wrong. She went out of the house immediately afterwards. I heard from Dr Pierse she was in the family-way, and that she had plenty of funds wherever they came from. He said, on my asking, that she had not told who the father was. The woman's daughter talked to the matron and to my wife, the schoolmistress.

John Irwin, master: I wish to add that when I made my report I did so from a sense of duty and not from any ill feeling.

Captain Hamilton: It was quite right the master should make a report. It was a great scandal that occurred.

To Mr Kavanagh: Why did you not report the circumstances sooner?

Kavanagh: I had no positive knowledge of Mary Murphy being pregnant till about a week before her confinement, when I was informed of it by Dr Pierse. I thought if I had reported it before admission of the child that it would be outside my sphere of duty, that I could not report it on an outside pauper.

Captain Hamilton: I consider it would be your duty to report it even though the child had not been admitted, if there was any suspicion of its having occurred in the house. It was your duty to clear the character of the house.

Mr Irwin: When Dr Pierse spoke to me about the matter, he said the woman had plenty of money, wherever it came from, but he said she did not mention a word about the paternity of the child.

Stephen Kavanagh, clerk: With regard to the letters referred to in the evidence, I was in the habit of often getting letters for Mary Murphy. The first letter was about getting a place for her child. The second was one sent to me for her. I get letters for other inmates of the house as well. I deny having had anything to say to Mary Murphy in the way of immorality or even having given her money, except a shilling at Christmas, which I was in the habit of giving the woman who cleaned up the office.

Mary Kelly: Mary Murphy lodged with me on Castle Street. She never made any statement to me regarding the father of her child, except one night she said laughing, the child should be called Thomas Furlong. I sent word to Fr Browne when she got bad. I stayed four nights with her, waked her and all and never got anything. She had plenty of money for her own wants during her illness, but I never got anything. I never heard her refer to the father only the once, but of course women can say what they like that way.

Miss Scallan, matron: Mary Murphy took her discharge. My duty was to search her. I was startled by her appearance and I spoke to the master who spoke to her. He said he did not think there was anything wrong. I said I was very glad. After she left the

Above left: Tony Parle was one of the founding members of one of the incarnations of Wexford Camera Club. Here he is seen snapping the harbour from the Woodenworks. (Rossiter Collection)

Above right: Nicky the 'ONE man'. The ONE here stands for the Organisation of National Ex-servicemen and women, of which Nicky was a proud and very active member. (Rossiter Collection)

house I heard she was in the family-way. I spoke to the porter who said she never was without money and that he always when he wanted her could find her in the board-room. Mary Murphy's illegitimate child is now in the workhouse. She herself is dead. I had some conversation with Sarah Murphy, who had been an inmate with her mother. Sarah Murphy was living at Quinn's in Barrack Street. The mother was at Kelly's, Castle Street, where she died. Sarah Murphy came for a coffin for her mother's body. She said the infant was alive and was called Thomas Furlong. She said she had got money from Johanna Sutton who got it from Mr Kavanagh. She herself had got £1 from Sutton, that her mother had got it at other times.

Mrs Irwin, schoolmistress: Mary Murphy's little girl, about 15 November, when I met her coming to the house, told me she was coming for money to Mr Kavanagh to give it to her mother. She told me where she was stopping. I asked why she stayed there and she asked me to get her out of it, that it was by her mother's wishes. I took her to the clergy, who got her into the House of Mercy.

WEXFORD PEOPLE

Where would a town or a history be without its people? In this volume we look at some people I knew and some that I only knew by reputation, who each added their threads to the tapestry that is Wexford.

GEORGE BRIDGES

For decades, George Bridges was our harbinger of Christmas. The summer excursions to Rosslare were only beginning to peter out when his little teasers began to appear in the notes sections of the local newspapers. The tag would be 'Sixteen weeks to Christmas', followed by a reminder to start planning, saving or 'putting things by'. This sort of Wexford Macy's emanated not from a huge multi-storey emporium but from a little shop in Selskar that was probably no more than ten feet wide and thirty feet deep, although he did have another outlet further up the street and expanded to opening a storeroom in Trimmers Lane as the fateful date approached.

A church dedicated to St Michael was located at the top of Castle Hill Street. This incorporated the Norse burial ground outside the walls. Burials continued there into the 1900s, with families who already had graves being interred.

George Bridges *was* Selskar and Christmas to many people. In a newspaper interview he recalled 200 years of Bridges' presence in that area of Wexford. His forefathers had been involved in the hire of horses, carts and sidecars from an address of 18 Selskar Street for centuries.

The familiar Bridges shop began as a sweet shop operated by Mary Elizabeth Bridges in 1920 and sold fruit and ice cream. Her husband Joseph was a barber and George recounts that a regular customer was M.J. O'Connor the solicitor, who had an appointment to be shaved in his own office at eight o'clock every morning.

George began his working life as an apprentice in Lipton's. This was a grocery store that survived into the 1960s and was probably a part of a British chain of which we had quite a number in Wexford. His wages on starting amounted to 13s 7d. It was in 1945 that he became more involved in the shop that would define him for Wexford people. He recalled travelling to the markets in Dublin seeking out new toys to enthrall the boys and girls of Wexford. As time progressed, the wholesale toy marketing was the domain of the bigger manufacturers and he ended up travelling to London to stock the famous Triang, Hornby and Meccanno toys. In addition to these, the shop was a Mecca for Matchbox and Dinky cars. These were collected, swapped, raced and treasured by generations. Many still, no doubt, grace the glass cabinets of doting grandfathers who recall that trip to Selskar with the few bob to spend hours looking, choosing, changing their mind and eventually carrying home that little vehicle in its cardboard box. Bridges closed its doors in 1994 but the shop and the man remain vivid in our memories of Wexford and Christmas.

BEN FENLON

Ben Fenlon was a major character in the 1940s and into the 1950s, but some of the tales about him may stretch credulity. We give them here as we found in research and recollection.

Ben and his brother Michael were men ahead of their times in the world of recycling. Their cries of 'Bottles, jam jars or clothes' drew hordes of young and not-so-young people into the battle for the planet — well, the battle for a few bob actually. Ben and Michael were not expecting anything for nothing and they actually paid you for your old bottles, jars and clothes, which of course they also would obtain money for. Prices were assigned by size and many a person financed their leisure activities by collecting bottles and jars in anticipation of the brothers' visits.

The story about Ben is that he was the grandson of another Michael. That Michael had arrived from Carlow with the militia and eventually settled in Black Cow Lane in Thomas Street and it was said that he fathered sixty children over

DIARMAID NA NGALL HENRI REX ROBERT FITZ STEPHEN CE GUR THARRAINGIOMAR SCRIOS AGUS EOLASMACHT AR EIRINN DO SNAISHERSIOMAR SHUR NOIDHREACHTI SHUR NOUCHAS SHUR MUINTI

This picture once adorned Gibson Street. It depicts the main protagonists in the Norman invasion of 1169. (Rossiter Collection)

three marriages. His first wife, Mary Ouselm, gave birth to twenty-four children. His second wife, Margaret Murphy had sixteen children, and later Mary Murphy from Ballinslaney would present him with another twenty children. Michael is said to have lived to the age of ninety-nine years and died on 11 January 1900. Although many of the children chose to leave Wexford, it was said that for one Christmas there were forty-three requiring dinner in the little family home. Michael was said to have initially supported the family by calling to houses of the poor and giving basic education in the so-called 'Three Rs'. He then set up as a general dealer. His last direct descendant was said to be George who passed away in 1948.

JAMES J. STAFFORD

James J. Stafford was born in South Main Street on 26 November 1860 to Patrick Stafford, who worked for Jasper Walsh & Company, timber merchants, at the Crescent. The family also had a small grocery store at South Main Street. James was educated at the Christian Brothers and his first employment was at the Wexford Dockyard where he rose to managerial rank.

In 1891, he purchased his first ships – the schooner *Mary and Gertrude* and the ketch *Zion Hill*. He continued to add to his fleet. In 1900, he went into the coal business, having purchased the premises of John E. Barry on Paul Quay. Stafford was to add furniture, hardware, funeral undertaking, a public house, electricity generation and more to the empire over the years that followed. In 1915, he bought a guest house in Trinity Street and expanded into adjoining premises as the Talbot Hotel. In 1918, he purchased the Wexford Timber Company that had existed in various guises at the Crescent since 1817. By 1928, he had a confectionary company producing jams and sweets known as 'Golden Crescent'.

In 1931, he had three companies: J.J. Stafford & Company, Wexford Timber Company and Wexford Steamship Company. He was also chairman of Irish Motor Ships Limited and Messrs P. Donnelly & Company of Dublin. He was involved in the Talbot Hotel and the Talbot Garage and is said that he was the first petrol stockist in Wexford.

In addition to the many business pursuits, Stafford was mayor of Wexford for three full terms at a time when being mayor was more than ceremonial. It also included the duty of Chief Magistrate and was one that was well placed for 'controlling the import and export trade'.

For us, growing up in Wexford in the 1950s, our contacts with Stafford's were mainly through going to Paul Quay to order coal, which would be delivered by that grey lorry and the sacks carried in by Tom Cleary. We also watched out for any rare appearances in their 'box' in the Capitol Cinema but I cannot ever recall seeing them there.

The Talbot Hotel, 1932.

The development in the background of this picture is on the old approach to the Old Bridge or Carcur Bridge out near Crosstown. Part of the old bridge is still visible. The area in the foreground has since been incorporated into the RNLI boathouse. It once gave access to 'The dead house', where bodies recovered from the harbour would be kept pending an inquest. (Rossiter Collection)

JOHN LOWNEY

Although a man of many talents, John Lowney is perhaps best known in Wexford for being one of the businessmen who helped people furnish their first home – or their few rooms as it was more likely in his early days. John left school at the age of fourteen to assist his father Joseph in a furniture business in Henrietta Street. Joseph was a cabinet maker and stories are told of young John regularly being 978 1 84588 993 7 seen delivering the finished articles on a trolley in those days before the delivery vans plied our streets. He left the bright lights of Wexford to try his luck in Enniscorthy but rather than settling there he brought back a bride – Peggy.

His other main talent was music, and with his brothers Joe and Tony, he formed a danceband and toured the country. In the early 1950s he had a plan that might have seen him rival the Albert Reynoldses of the showband era. He bought some land at Ferrybank and was intent on building a dancehall and entertainment complex. This was four years before the present bridge even opened and access would have been via Carcur and Crosstown, which made the venture very far sighted and ambitious. At the request of no less than the bishop, who was concerned about 'fear of young ladies' safety', he abandoned the idea – but not the music. Instead, he transferred his ambition to Redmond Hall in Spawell Road, where the husband and wife team managed a venue that improved the romantic life of young Wexford. A story is told that a regular serenade at Redmond Hall on a Sunday night was Dan Kelly singing 'Danny Boy' for the adjacent convent dwellers of St John of God.

Paradise Row was home to the family of Thomas D'Arcy Magee, who was to find fame in Canada in the 1800s. Canadian tourists wishing to find the homestead are not in for much luck. The remains of Paradise Row are under weeds and briars between the houses of Waterloo Road and Corry's Villas, going down to the Presentation sports field. (Rossiter Collection)

In this historic picture of North Main Street from over a century ago, we see horse power was at its peak. The extreme left may show the remnants of the Tholsel at the Bullring.

In 1956, Lowney decided to concentrate his efforts once more on furniture and opened his first Wexford shop at 61 South Main Street. Within a few years they had acquired the adjoining premises and expanded to become the Universal Stores. That was in the late 1960s and their furniture store covered a floor area almost unheard of in a provincial town. The business grew and expanded into other areas such as electricals, televisions and everything to make a house a home, as the saying goes. Never one to sit still, he sought other business opportunities. He opened an auction room that drew large crowds, no doubt entertained by a man well used to performance. He later turned the Long Room public house, which had been Wickham's Brewery in the past, into a large snooker club attracting world class-players and tournaments to Wexford. The businesses still thrive but I suppose it is in true Wexford back-handed compliment tradition that we often forget the person, although his name lives on as we refer to Lowney's Mall as if it were an ancient thoroughfare from medieval days.

SAMUEL BYRNE

Samuel Byrne was born in 1810, the son of John Byrne, married to Esther Fortune and later Ann Atkin, who had a Brazier Foundry employing over fifty people in Foundry Lane (later Patrick's Lane). Samuel was indentured as an apprentice to Ambrose Fortune, a watchmaker, for seven years. Fortune's shop was located at 57 North Main Street. It later became Richard's.

Byrne finished that apprenticeship on 27 October 1832 at the age of twenty-two. He was attested as 'very clever at restaining jewellery'. He opened his own business at 50 South Main Street as a master clock maker and jeweller. He died of a stroke in his store on 7 December 1858. His wife, Mary Moore Byrne managed the shop for eighteen years before eventually selling it and emigrating to Canada.

CAPTAIN THOMAS WALSH

Known as 'Lannigan' by everyone, Captain Thomas Walsh was born in 3 William Street and was often described as 'the father of Wexford's sailors'. He was the son of Captain James Walsh, who died of fever on board the Barque *Kate*, of which he was skipper.

Lannigan first went to sea at the age of thirteen and a half and stayed active in marine careers up to the age of sixty-eight. He attained his Master Mariner's Certificate at the age of twenty-one. His first command was *The Rambler*. During his long career he sailed as Master on about fifty-three vessels including *Ellen Kerr*, *Jane McCall*, *Yarra Yarra*, *Wave*, and *Mary Agnes*. The final vessel he sailed on was the *A. Hastings*, a two-masted schooner. At one time he was a commander in the Wexford fleet of sailing ships known as the *Galatzmen*, whose epic races home from the Black Sea with grain and cargoes were as famous in those days as those of the China clippers.

Black-bearded Captain Walsh was the holder of the coveted Square-rigged Master's certificate. A hard-driving, fearless navigator of the days of wooden ships and 'iron men', Lannigan could boast after such a life at sea that he never lost a ship. He is recalled as a genial companion who took a keen interest in current affairs. He was lucky enough to enjoy excellent health throughout his life. His picture appeared as the frontispiece of a book called *Songs of the Wexford Coast* by Fr Joseph Ranson in 1948, to which he contributed a number of shanties. He was at one time the oldest member of the Holy Family Confraternity as a Gold Jubilarian. He had ten sons and three daughters, forty-eight grandchildren and fifty-three great-grandchildren.

MICHAEL JOSEPH O'CONNOR

O'Connor was a merchant who was born in Wexford in 1835. At one stage he lived at 3 Lower George Street. A niece of his was Minnie O'Connor, who built the eight red-brick houses at Glena Terrace. Minnie O'Connor carried on the building trade of her father and grandfather Timothy O'Connor and Patrick O'Connor. Michael Joseph O'Connor served his time as an apprentice to Patrick O'Connor, building a church at Curracloe, when he met Johanna Murphy.

Johanna Murphy, daughter of James Murphy of Curracloe, was born in 1841 and married Michael Joseph O'Connor on 9 February 1863 in the parish church at Castlebridge. This was the old church which was behind Nunn's Mill and is no longer there, the new church at Castlebridge having been subsequently built.

They lived in North Main Street, Wexford, where they opened a bakery and dwelt above. In 1868, they extended their premises and carried on a very successful bakery business. Their children were born in the premises over the bakery and were called 'the baker's dozen'.

Avenue de Flandres was built by Pierces in the late 1930s and named after the location of their Paris office. Pierces built a number of housing projects at the time and this one was primarily used to house upper management. (Rossiter Collection)

Clarence House.
The original
Clarence
buildings were
built in 1830 on
the site of Bishop
Caulfield's palace.
It was at one time
the residence
of the Sisters of
Mercy Nuns.
In the 1800s,
seven houses and
a garden here
were to be sold
via lottery of
450 tickets at £3
3s each. Tickets
did not sell
and the lottery
was postponed.
(Rossiter
Collection)

M.J. O'CONNOR

M.J. O'Connor married Catherine Wickham in Ballymore. The marriage is also recorded in the parish register of Rowe Street, Wexford. It was a double wedding – Catherine Wickham's sister married Paddy Hickey from New Ross the same day. M.J. and Catherine lived first in the last house in Glena Terrace and then they moved up to Westlands in or around 1914.

M.J. O'Connor was educated by the Jesuits at Tullabeg and studied to become a solicitor. He had been apprenticed to Martin Huggard, solicitor. An indenture of apprenticeship of 1883 states that M.J.'s father joined in the apprenticeship deed to confirm that he would be responsible for M.J.'s behaviour as an apprentice to Martin Huggard.

When qualified, O'Connor started a practice at George Street, in the premises reputed to have been the town house of Bagenal Harvey. In 1894, the premises was rebuilt by Mary Ann O'Connor and was said to be the first purpose-built solicitor's office in the country. He proceeded to open up branch offices in Arklow, Coolgreaney and Gorey.

He was involved in several well-known cases but his chief claim to fame is his involvement with the Land Purchase Acts. On the passing of the Ashbourne Land Act in 1888, he negotiated on behalf of tenants the first sale under that statute. A series of articles contributed to *The Free Press* under the pen name of B.L. attracted the attention of Mr George Wyndham, the Chief Secretary for Ireland, who in 1903 introduced in the House of Commons a New Land Act which incorporated some of M.J.'s proposals and recommendations. The passing of this measure by the British Parliament resulted in the sale of several estates throughout Ireland which would

In 1918, Wexford witnessed one of its largest funerals ever. The death of John Redmond, leader of the Irish Party at Westminster, cast a black cloud over the area. Redmond had come closer than anyone to bringing Home Rule to Ireland by peaceful means. He was buried at the family vault in John Street graveyard. (Rossiter Collection)

not have been negotiated were it not for the bonus scheme. One of O'Connor's big achievements was the completion of the sale of the estate of the late John E. Redmond. When Dáil Éireann decided to appoint a commission to examine the land question of the Free State, M.J. O'Connor was asked by Mr P. Hogan, the Minister for Agriculture, to act as one of its members.

He was also one of the first workers in the Gaelic Movement in County Wexford and one of the three delegates from the county who attended the convention in Thurles at which the Gaelic Athletic Association was established. He was the prime mover in the organisation of sports in Wexford held under the auspices of the popular National Organisation of Athletics in the country. He was a member of the famous Blue and Whites Club which brought renown to Wexford town and county for many years. He was honorary secretary of the North Slob races and in 1902 was presented by the committee with a silver salver as a token of his valuable help in the organisation of the fixtures. He took a keen interest in deep-sea fishing and the foundation of the Gannett Fishing Company which operated in Wexford about forty years ago. It was also mainly through his efforts that the North and South Sloblands were made preserves for wildfowl and are today one of the most popular trysting places of shoots in the country.

FINTAN O'CONNOR

Born at Ballask Carne in 1900, in Keating's house, Fintan O'Connor was baptised by Fr Whitty PP. He attended Loreto kindergarten. His memories included Canon Luke Doyle in Tagoat, who did not like ladies to cycle to Mass as their ankles were exposed. He went to Clongowes Wood College in 1914. He recalled soldiers on station during the war and also guards on tunnels and banks during the War of Independence/Civil War. O'Connor had a gas producer on his motor car during the 1939/45 war. The car's number was MI 5209. He also recalled that Drinagh was a common landing place for aeroplanes.

SIR JAMES O'CONNOR

Sir James O'Connor began his career in law in 1894 as a solicitor in partnership with his brother M.J. Abandoning the solicitor's profession, James was called to the Irish Bar at Michaelmas 1900, at the age of twenty-eight years and he built up an extensive and lucrative practice. He was called to the Inner Bar in 1908, after which he figured in many notable cases.

Left: Take note of the ornate door and the sadly necessary barred windows on this little house which survived the development of the historic Well Lane. Well Lane was previously called Bolan's Lane. In the 1800s there were fourteen houses listed here. (Rossiter Collection)

Below: This picture dates from the time when this was Smith's & Renault cars were being assembled here. The crates visible in the compound were the ones in which parts arrived. Most of these eventually became garden sheds throughout Wexford – an early example of recycling. (Rossiter Collection)

The end of Duke's Lane. This wonderfully named lane disappeared in the 1960s. We never knew it as anything other than Duke's Lane but earlier references called it Duke's Street. Count Sarsfield Lucan died at Duke Street, Wexford on 4 September 1817. (Rossiter Collection)

When the Solicitor Generalship for Ireland became vacant in 1914 he was appointed to fill the vacancy. He became Attorney General for Ireland in l917. In that capacity he advised the government strongly against conscription for Ireland and tendered his resignation at this point. He was given a position in the Court of Appeal when he was then only forty-six years of age. In the course of his busy career he found time to write the well-known textbooks *The Licensing Laws of Ireland*, *Motor Car Acts* and *The Irish Justice of the Peace*. He also wrote a *History of Ireland, 1798 to l924*.

In 1922, O'Connor was appointed Chairman of the Railway Commission under the Provisional Government in Ireland and acted as Chairman of the Irish Coal Commission, and arbitrated on several trade disputes. He became a member of the Privy Council. He married in 1925. On his retirement from the position of Lord Justice of Appeal when he was fifty-two years of age, he went to reside in England and decided to practice at the Bar in that country, where he had been a King's Counsel since 1925. He was also very keen on sports. He was involved in many clubs and was President of Milltown Golf Club for many years.

Devereux Villas is named after Richard Devereux, businessman, ship owner and philanthropist of the nineteenth century. The houses were built by Wexford Corporation and named in 1941. Note the tiny wheels on the pram and the two children being transported. (Courtesy of Kiernan/Scanlon Collection)

STREETS

In *The Streets of Wexford* I avoided the main shopping area because the task of tracing the history of the shops and buildings seemed be virtually impossible. But many people have asked that I make some stab at it so here goes.

NORTH MAIN STREET

For most of us, North Main Street starts at what used to be Joyce's at the top of Anne Street. For me, Main Street started there in the late 1960s, when I went to work in the front hardware section of the shop with Pat Sullivan, Joe Fallon and Martin Cleere. We were located just inside the front door selling teapots, crockery, cutlery and the like. Our immediate boss was Pat White, affectionately known as 'GAA' because of his passion for Gaelic games. He had a little office under the stairs shared on occasion with the boss, Murt Joyce. The main memory of those early days in Joyce's was of dusting, polishing and rearranging the goods. Then there was stocktaking, or replenishing the displays, when we had to go to the top floors of the building to the store rooms for kettles, pots, pans, companion sets and new ranges of cups and saucers.

Joyce's was divided into a number of departments at the time and up a short set of steps from our section was the paint shop where Padge Reck and at one time Jimmy Flynn worked. Upstairs were white goods such as kitchen appliances and also an electrical department selling everything from fuses to stereos. There was also a repair section there. Among the employees upstairs were Margaret Paige, Des Troy and Tommy Tierney. There was a gas store in Anne Street and another larger one on The Quay. Giving an indication of the stock carried, Joyce's also had storage in the old Employment Exchange that once stood on the north side of Anne Street. Kathleen Doyle presided over another outpost of Joyce's in the China Shop, where we had to tread very carefully among the Waterford Crystal, bone china and other expensive wedding present and presentation wares.

Between the two Joyce's outlets on North Main Street were some interesting places. The first was the Mechanic's Institute. It dated originally from the mid-1800s but in to the twentieth century it was used mainly for union meetings and the like. I think it was the Amalgamated Engineering Union that used the upstairs room to collect union dues on Friday nights from operatives employed in Pierce's.

Another institution on this part of the street was *People* Newspapers, or as we called it the *People* Office. This was the retail office for the newspaper and for the

This picture from the 1970s reminds us of some of the shops now gone from North Main Street. The youngster is sitting on the window of Godkin's, a major retailer who also supplied grain and feedstuffs from stores stretching up to Back Street. Kirby's Chemist is long gone, as is Jenkin's, one of our first home-grown department stores. (Rossiter Collection)

Ireland's Own, where advertisements were taken in. The office led to the printing works on High Street via steps in what was once Archer's Lane.

Further along North Main Street was another shop where I eventually worked. It was The Book Centre and its first Wexford location was beside Hassett's, that part where the street suddenly narrowed. When I worked in Joyce's we frequented the same location but for sausage and chips rather than books when it was the original Fortes.

Eating features significantly in the memories of this part of the Main Street. Opposite Corry's, which was advertised as 130 years old in 1955, was Nangle's and later M & J's restaurant. There had been a popular bakery on one of the sites earlier.

Beside what was the Corish Memorial Hall was the watering hole of many a canvasser for the Labour Party in the Tower Bar (or the Oak Lounge as it had been before that).

Past Church Lane is St Iberius church and directly opposite that was Jenkin's department store. This stretched over a number of buildings and sold just about everything you might need, from the famous or infamous Clarke's sandals with the T-strap and crepe sole that adorned every child's foot in the summer months, to a dining-room suite in the newlyweds' flat. The office in Jenkin's was a regular stop for the children doing the messages on a Saturday morning to pay a few shillings on the book. Sam Coe was the main man in that office for many years.

Another of the multinational shops in Wexford into the 1960s was the Home & Colonial Stores, where a tiled floor was often covered with a sprinkling of sawdust. That appears to have been the common practice in shops selling meat at the time, as many butchers had a similar practice. Lipton's was another such store selling groceries.

Sullivan's was a shop that I have little recollection of entering, but it was certainly impressive by its pillared entrance. Across from there was Jack Fane's, one of the quintessential pub-come-grocery stores of the 1950s. For some reason, probably a Castlebridge connection to my Walsh ancestors, we bought a lot of our groceries there and it was a main port of call on Saturday mornings. Just inside the front door on the right was an elevator connecting to the cellar where, like many such pubs at the time, they bottled their own stout. To the left was the snug. This little cubicle was where the ladies could have a quiet drink without being noticed. The grocery section stretched along from there to a door leading into the bar. There were no lounges at that time. One of the regulars in Jack Fane's was Jackie Culleton. He was my first dentist and had his practice upstairs in one of the adjoining buildings. Apparently he was a bit of a GAA hero and had the manner and bulk to match, so a visit to the dentist was not relished.

Passing over the Bullring we would have encountered the Ritz Café, part of the Frank O'Connor food empire. There was also Love's Café opposite and Cooke's shop, where I think I can recall was a travel agent in the infancy of such things and a firearms dealership.

Bullring Bazaar, 1900. This old photograph gives the date of the event as 3-4 September 1900.
We can see the good-sized gas lamps that would have lighted the public streets of the era. The
absence of 'The Pikeman' confirms a date prior to 1904 but its location was obviously booked,
as we can see from the pikes in circles on the two gable walls of the market place. (Courtesy of
Kiernan/Scanlon Collection)

Hadden's, later Shaw's, was another of our department stores. It was the first 'fixed
price' store in Wexford dating back many decades. Murphy's chemist was also along
here. This was a great place for budding photographers in the 1960s. It was there
that I remember buying the 'gear' to develop black and white films and print my
first photographs. The developing tank was a black plastic drum that the film was
transferred to in total darkness. My father built me a little darkroom in a corner of the
bedroom to facilitate this hobby. He had dabbled in photography with the old box
brownies some decades before and had also developed his own snaps. Initially we made
contact prints by placing the developed negative directly on the paper, exposing it and
developing and fixing it. Later, we progressed to enlarging to 'en-print' size. This was
achieved with an oblong enlarger – a metal box with a lens – that gave us postcard-size
prints. We then progressed to a real enlarger and must have nearly suffocated people
with the pong of developers and fixers emanating from the 'darkroom'.

Matt Murphy was a great asset to any aspiring photographer of the day. He often had old stock of 127 or 620 film that he let you have at a good price and this was a great encouragement to experiment before we moved on to the 'professional' 35mm cameras and films. He also encouraged us into the colour slide option as we referred to transparencies. The slide projector was 'the thing' for the good colour holiday shots at a time when holidays were just becoming popular. How visitors' hearts must have plummeted as the host said, 'Would you like to see the holiday slides?', prefacing an hour of pictures of people you never knew in places you had no interest in.

As North Main Street narrowed again, heading towards Selskar, we had Walker's and then White's Hotel with its famous coffee shop. That was the most popular venue for young people throughout the late 1960s and into the 1970s. There, Margaret Hearne presided over the newly acquired taste for coffee – ironically our first smell of coffee had come from Walker's just up the street – or the bottle of coke that was made to last for hours.

Bullring to the Gut, 1950s. What would become Sloans and eventually be demolished to widen the access to Cornmarket was still Hyne's General Drapery Store. There are three horses and carts parked at the kerb, which are probably collecting supplies from Godkin's, whose shop is just out of sight. (Courtesy of Kiernan/Scanlon Collection)

This 'in-between' picture shows an interim version of White's Hotel that existed for only a few years in the late 1900s. It was part of the structure that had extended the old coaching inn and was later to become the local library, before demolition to make way for the present structure. (Rossiter Collection)

Still thinking of food, the first Chinese restaurant I remember in Wexford was Wong's or Michael's. Part of the exotic ambiance was the illuminated fish tank incorporated into the wall. Although it was a Chinese restaurant, we always seemed to order the more European or even Irish fare on the menu.

The building housing McCormack's chemist shop is reputed to have had its rent bequeathed to Wexford Corporation by none other than George Bernard Shaw.

Bridges shop is dealt with elsewhere in the book.

In the Selskar area of North Main Street was the Imperial Bar, formerly the Imperial Hotel. Prior to it burning down a few decades ago, this was the rock music venue for the youth of the town as opposed to the pop fans.

Another fire victim in the late 1900s was O'Brien's furniture store in Selskar. My main memory of this shop (called 'Jap O'Brien's' for some unknown reason) was the Christmas Santa, where you went to chat, pay your few bob and get a wrapped present.

SOUTH MAIN STREET

Drifting back in time and space over a few decades I can recall some of the shops and characters that inhabited Wexford's Main Street.

At the corner of Stonebridge Lane, where the motor factor shop now stands, there was once a smaller shop. Initially it had been Cullimore's but many who were in school in the 1960s will remember it as Morgan's. Mr Morgan had been in management in Pierce's before branching into the retail book and stationery trade. The shop always seemed cluttered, with no law or order on the contents. He did not carry much in the book line, but then very few did in those days, before the really cheap paperback and the specialist bookshop.

Lambert Place is often called Bunker's Hill, but in 1840 that street had not been opened and our Michael Street was then called Bunker's Hill. (Courtesy of Kiernan/Scanlon Collection)

Lost Lane was originally gated, then the gate was boarded up and eventually the opening disappeared completely. As Roman Lane it connected the quays to North Main Street beside what became the new Shaw's building. Even in the late twentieth century it could only be viewed through an iron gate on the quay end. (Rossiter Collection)

Andy Nolan had a vegetable shop almost opposite this at one time and there was another such shop on the western side. I think it was called the General Stores but for some reason the locals had their own name for it, christened from a popular television cartoon series.

An indication of the popularity of music making and pop groups is attested to the fact that Noel Randall could open a retail music shop here. Hayes (we pronounced it Hayeses) and Kavanagh had a popular bicycle shop along here at a time when for most of us the two-wheel transport was as much as we might aspire to. They also sold fishing bait. Further along was Kelly's Dairy and then McGrail's drapery shop. On the other side we had Eddie Slevin's electrical contractor and retail lighting shop. Paddy Carey's pub was opposite Bride Street and Barry's fish shop was beside it, selling the best of Rosslare herrings. Broader's, Travers's, Bugler Doyle's and the like were pub names opposite that corner. I recall going into one of them – no naming which – at lunchtime for a sandwich and the barman popping out to buy a sliced pan to facilitate the transaction.

John North was a popular hairdresser at South Main Street near Coffin Corner. He later moved to King Street. (Courtesy of Kiernan/Scanlon Collection)

This old postcard of South Main Street is dominated by the shop of S&R Pierce. The bustling street has two-way traffic. Signs above shops offer White Paraffin, Pye televisions and Sweet Afton cigarettes.

This was certainly the fishy end of town because Malone's fish shop was at the corner of Oyster Lane. Mr Malone usually had a big delph plate in the window – blue willow pattern I think – and more often than not the family cat was perched on it sunning herself.

On the Bride Street side was Coffin Corner, with a three-storey red-brick town house. I cannot recall it as a residence but do remember one of the many Tontine societies using the lower front rooms every Saturday to collect money. Next door used to be Denis O'Connor's studio, where many a scabby knee was photographed in short-trousered First Holy Communion suits on the days that were in it. Above the studio lived Marty Murphy, the brain that propelled many young Wexford men into business or accountancy. He was the teacher of bookkeeping and business methods in the CBS secondary school in Green Street. He always wore a three-piece suit and a hat outside class and was forever enquiring after Canon Murphy out in Glynn from any pupils from that area.

Aidan Kelly had a butcher shop next door and I seem to recall Tom Furlong – later of the Bullring – working for him. Beside this was the public convenience at the corner of the appropriately named Mann's Lane. A man nicknamed 'Sugar Al' worked there in the days of fully attended toilet facilities.

The Pettit's retail empire started in a shop across the road from here at Oyster Lane. It grew from a small shop in 1947 to a mini-supermarket, before they expanded to pastures new and eventually closed the South Main Street branch.

Then came the parish hall – officially the Dun Mhuire. This was our Mecca for pantomime, dancing, record hops, bingo (for the Ma), jumble sales, Tops of the Town, concerts by international stars, the drama festival in Lent when dancing was prohibited, and a hundred other entertainments including roller discos. Upstairs there were meetings of the Catholic Girls' Club, the Legion of Mary, Alcoholics Anonymous, the Holy Family Confraternity Band and others.

Next door was Alf Cadogan's, where you could get electrical goods, bicycles, tricycles and a multitude of other items. It later became Jim Crowley's paint shop.

This picture shows the junction of South Main Street and Peter's Street when Shudall's was the shop on the corner. God knows what that lady is doing with the brush, but the person in the shop door is keeping an eye on her. (Courtesy of Kiernan/Scanlon Collection)

This view of South Main Street has a number of interesting features, not least the tricycle in the foreground. It may be a simple delivery device or possibly a specialised ice-cream vendor. Harvey's is the shop on the left. Osborne's Select Bar is on the right just beyond Oyster Lane.

Opposite, there were shops like Kirby's chemists and Kelly's hair salon – there was a shop out front that you passed through to get the 'short back and sides' that was obligatory before The Beatles and their mop cuts became popular.

Johnny Murphy's Goal Bar was also on this stretch of street. It was a very popular location for GAA aficionados. One older institution here was Kevin Roche's. This was the old-style chip shop where you could take away or sit in after the night at the pictures. They served chips, fish, mushy peas, pig's feet, minerals and little else, in newsprint or on enamel plates. The long playbills for the three cinemas provided the reading material.

Coleman Doyle began his expansion along here, with a catchphrase for those seeking anything from a needle to an anchor of, 'If I haven't got it I will get it for you.' Across the road the Lowney juggernaut shifted into gear from small beginnings to occupy a huge store that stretched from Main Street almost to the quay, at a time when most shops were about a 'house deep'. Their furniture provided the necessities and home comforts to thousands of Wexford couples starting out on married life – often 'bought on the book'.

This old postcard of South Main Street is interesting for the box on the right, which denotes the building that would become the Dun Mhuire or Parish Hall in the early 1960s. With cars on both sides and the horse and cart, the street looks deceptively wide.

Other pubs in this corner included Heffernan's and Nick Murphy's, the preferred haunt of *The Free Press* staff for after work or a 'do' for someone who was leaving or getting married, when the 'wallop a notes' was handed over amid the flowing drinks. Across Cinema Lane was Eddie Hall's pub. Directly opposite Hall's was Shudall's sweet shop. I recall this little shop of about eight feet by twenty, with a counter down the right as you entered and a bench or form on the left wall under a mirror. An elderly lady owned the shop but most of the service was by Angie Molloy. It was the place to stock up on sweets before heading to the Cinema Palace.

Coffey's was a Wexford institution in the 1960s, as it had been for decades. In 1939, Coffey's advertising offered 'the greatest bargains ever experienced', including pianos, cycles, prams, clothing and diamond rings. It was the place for shoes, boots, clothes, bedding and nursery requisites. Initially presided over by Herbie and later his son Ray, it was one of the friendliest stores you might enter. The most memorable aspect of Coffey's was 'approbation', a word we understood only from our parents' interpretation. This was where you could choose shoes, clothes, etc., from the comfort of your own home. It probably grew from a time when the gentry got such a privilege but was later seen as essential when those shy factory and foundry workers may have balked at going to a shop to try on clothes. The messenger boy on his big 'high Nelly' bike with its square basket would deliver a selection of items to the home. There they would be tried on – usually with a multitude of opinions on offer from the extended family and possibly neighbours – until the ideal was chosen. The others were parcelled up for collection. The desired item or items was then 'put on the book' – a small red-covered notebook – and paid off at a few bob a week. This was the financial services section in action in the 1960s, when most stores serviced their own form of credit. Such stores also provided much-needed weekend employment to young people. Up Coffey's Hill – which had its own tune composed for the Boys' Band – was Wallace's. This was higher-class tailoring, with measuring, fitting, etc. This was the place for that special suit.

Nick Murphy's was a popular pub for staff of *The Free Press*. (Courtesy of Kiernan/Scanlon Collection)

This row of shops on South Main Street, near the junction with Cinema Lane, recalls another era, not least by the combination of mini and maxi skirts on the young ladies looking at Paddy Lacey's NPL Photos. Olde & Newe was a bric-a-brac shop that also stocked second-hand books and The Casket, with its wooden grill indicating a Sunday morning picture, sold everything from sweets to knitwear items. (Courtesy of Kiernan/Scanlon Collection)

Cinema Lane was officially Harpur's Lane, but it was seldom (if ever) called that by a genuine local. By the time this shot was taken the old Cinema Palace was gone, replaced by Roche's paint shop. The old sign would last a few more years. (Courtesy of Kiernan/Scanlon Collection)

Buckland's was on the same side in my day, although I understand it had started life on the other side of South Main Street. May and Ita were the occupiers in the 1960s. Again, this was a very small shop. As you entered there were newspapers to your right, then weekly comics and magazines on the wide counter, with sweets underneath. The books were shelved to your left. To the rear were the 'classy comics' – the Classic Illustrated, Dell, DC Comics and the sixty-four-page War Library range. Here we delved into the adventures of Batman, Superman and the other superheroes of the magical USA. Such comics were for special occasions or when we had that extra few bob after doing a few messages. The bread-and-butter comics were *The Topper*, *The Beezer*, *The Dandy*, *The Beano* and the like, which the parents usually bought on a weekly basis as a regular treat. There was a science to this purchasing. It had to be controlled so that there was swap market potential, so parents were usually instructed what to buy and what to avoid because one of our friends had it on order. Commodity trading had nothing on us in those days.

Beside Buckland's was the Singer sewing machine shop and opposite was a greengrocer on the corner of Henrietta Street. Yet another home-grown retail giant started out on this bit of South Main Street. It was Johnny Hore's. It started in the 1940s and was quite unusual in its advertising in that Mr Hore was a bit of a poet and placed eagerly awaited rhyming adverts in the local newspapers.

Woolhead's.

Nolan's, on the corner of Allen Street, was a hub of teenage activity in the early days of teenagers. It had a jukebox and a pool table and was a sort of unofficial youth club on most days and nights of the week, behind its red façade. Paddy Lyons had a shoe shop that is said to have introduced the printed plastic carrier bag to Wexford.

Woolworth's has been recorded before but what about the shop next door – a similar name but no relation. That was Woolhead's, one of the major attractions for young and old throughout the year, but especially at Christmas. Its Aladdin's Cave was filled with all manner of exotic and unusual treats to part the young people from the pocket money that was becoming fashionable at the time. Children would be at their wit's end trying to decide what to buy and at times they let fate take a hand by purchasing a wrapped surprise parcel.

Beside here was the Radio Store. This was Nicky Hore's and it was the place for radiograms – the big lump of furniture with a radio and a record player cunningly concealed inside. He also sold televisions as the craze took off and had a small record selection. Looking at the amount of music on offer today, it's amazing how we survived in the 1960s with a free-standing rack of LPs and the limited new releases of six-inch singles.

N.J. or Nicky Hore's Radio House spanned the entrance to Slegg's Lane (the opening in the middle). As the picture shows, it was not only radios or even electrical goods that he sold. There were Hercules bicycles, the ubiquitous tansad, tennis rackets, low-slung prams and fridges. (Courtesy of Kiernan/Scanlon Collection)

Slegg's Lane is the seaward extension of Keysar's Lane. It is entered via a low arch opposite Fitzgerald's shop. One then descends a short flight of steps under the shops to emerge into a car park. In earlier timer one would continue down the narrow thoroughfare to the Deep Pool or Crescent Quay. In October 1866, this lane was one of three mentioned as being in a filthy state and a danger to public health, with cholera in the town. (Rossiter Collection)

In a big red-fronted shop at the corner of Keyser's Lane we had S&R Pierce who sold hardware, seeds and guns and ammunition. Across the lane was Imco, cleaners and dyers, where you got your clothes cleaned and/or dyed in those pre-built-in obsolescence days.

The relics of oul' decency existed into the 1960s and indeed well into the 1990s; the shop opposite Imco was called The L&N Tea Company and it would later move to Church Lane, where it would remain until it changed to SuperValu. What we may forget is that the full title was The London & Newcastle Tea Company, betraying its colonial origins.

Next door was Dunnes Stores, where we once had Healy & Collins, famed for its overhead docket propelling system. Across from here was Ally White's, yet one more sweet shop, but this also offered ice cream sundaes and orange sodas. They sold a lovely spearmint bar that my mother was semi-addicted to. It had no name on the wrapper, just a sort of spider-web design. It was here we also scoffed Macaroon Bars and Flash Bars.

Above: Here we see Healy
& Collins at its height, with
stores on either side of the
Main Street. Note the large
glass frontage on the first-floor
right. Ally White's is just along
from there. The Central Bar
is on the left, with M.J. or
Matty Furlong's opposite. This
was an emporium to rival the
big department stores, selling
wallpaper, stationery and even
musical instruments.

Left: These red-brick
buildings were part of the
Stafford holdings around
Stonebridge. The end building
was demolished a few years
back and a new structure
replaced the lovely arched
windows. It was Corcoran's
turf accountants at one time
in the 1970s and later Frank
Cullimore's was opposite
it, across the lane entrance.
(Rossiter Collection)

Mayor Eddie Hall opened the new premises of RTV Rentals in 1961, on the eve of Ireland's first television station. Wexford had entered the television age. In those prudent days very few people would consider buying a television. Renting was the norm for your accommodation, so why not do the same with the telly? Okay you never owned it, but you nor did you have to pay for repairs – and call outs were a big thing in those days. It seemed like every other week the children sat staring out the window waiting for the 'RTV man' to come and fix the telly. The public telephone boxes would be buzzing with calls to Fergie Morris at RTV looking for a service call when the screen had gone blank, the picture kept 'rolling' or the 'thing was all snowy'.

Rochford's was another drapery shop that was popular at the time. Donal Howlin was the assistant there. Across from here was Harry Stone's, a grocery and public house, and beside that was the Wexford Gas Consumers Company. Dunnes had started out in the building on the corner of Anne Street.

STONEBRIDGE

The hundred or so yards from the original Stonebridge to the corner of King Street was a bit like Las Vegas or Soho. The top of Sinnott's Lane was flanked by two bookies; there was a cinema, a gaming emporium, a 'soda fountain' style hangout with tobacco and knives on sale, and a few pubs.

The bookies (or bookmakers or turf accountants) were Frank Cullimore and Corcoran. My clearest recollections are of Cullimore's, where me Ma placed her bets. Those were the days before liberalisation, when children were banned, live broadcasts of the events were not allowed, and horses and maybe dogs were the only objects of bets. The banning of under-eighteens was a problem when the adults could not get downtown. This was overcome by sending the children with the betting slip wrapped around the money. They darted into Rosie or Nancy then went and waited outside the door for the docket to be brought out. The windows of those and other bookies always caught the eyes of those heading home from work, as they checked the winners and losers of the day. Cullimore's later became Louis Codd's, then Nancy Codd's and finally a branch of a chain. Corcoran's was demolished in the early part of this century.

The gaming emporium was the Granada Grill, or as most Wexford people called it, 'Joe Dillon's'. It served food and had a few slot machines on the ground floor. It was upstairs that it flourished as a bingo hall, one of very few private enterprise bingo halls in the county (most were parish or community enterprises). Not that the Granada bingo, which ran three nights a week, did not have a charitable status –

it was run in aid of the Loch Garman Silver Band and drew excellent crowds. The patrons had a full gambling week with only Saturday off. The other venues were the parish hall on Sunday, Camross on Thursday, and Taghmon, or later Clonard, on another night.

The 'soda fountain' was O'Toole's, where young people could linger for hours over a bottle of mineral or later that wild cup of coffee. Ironically, in a building where so many young people congregated, the other primary merchandise (apart from toy cars) was cigarettes, cigars and Swiss army knives.

To add to the 'Sin City' reputation, we could add that Stonebridge was the scene of Wexford's first recorded murder case in 1560.

QUAYS

Despite the grandeur of the promenade and the magnificent view out over the harbour, the Wexford Quays of today are but a pale imitation of their former glory, industry and importance.

Imagine tall, four-masted schooners anchored in the bay waiting for berths. Picture the hustle and bustle on the quays as cargoes that originated in all ports of the world were unloaded and the produce of Wexford and its hinterland awaited shipment to Barbados, Odessa or West Africa. The air was filled with the aroma of spices mixed with more earthy smells; a dozen foreign tongues filled the ear and the constant sound of industry resonated.

The long line of quays in Wexford only date from the early 1800s. Prior to that, like most ports, there was a series of wharfs of varying length and width jutting out into the harbour. These were privately built and operated and usually bore the names of the owners of the businesses they served. Many such names would later transfer to the lanes that ran along to original line of the wharf.

The quays, from the time of reconstruction into the 1900s, were a separate domain. They were administered by the Wexford Harbour Commissioners and had their own police force of harbour constables. Many of the current streets heading from Main Street to the quays were actually closed and locked at sunset in those days and did not reopen until dawn. To all intents and purposes, Wexford Quays were an enclosed working space much like the docks of major ports. The quayfront was not a promenade and there was no space, entitlement, or desire to go for a stroll in such an area.

The early history of many of the buildings on the quays is difficult to trace because so many were warehouses, sawmills or stores. The quay proper travelling from the south starts with a pub, and why not, in the 1900s the whole quay was

Left: A popular destination for a Sunday afternoon family walk was Ferrycarrig. The more energetic might even try the round trip through Castlebridge returning via the Carcur Bridge, or later along the New Bridge. Adding the small bridge at Castlebridge this was called 'doing the three bridges'. The line of this road has been altered completely since this 1940s picture. (Courtesy of Kiernan/ Scanlon Collection)

Below: This shot from the 1970s shows the re-alignment of the main road at Ferrycarrig and gives some indication of the excavation work undertaken. (Rossiter Collection)

Above: The *Guillemot* opened on Wexford Quay in July 1968. It was the first use of a former lightship as a museum in Europe. (Rossiter Collection)

Opposite above: Crab fishing was one of the 'everyman' sports during the many regattas that dotted the Sunday afternoons of Wexford up to the 1960s. All that was needed was a bit of line and a few mussels – plus a bit of space on the Woodenworks. Prizes were on offer for the biggest specimen and most caught. (Rossiter Collection)

Opposite below: This is Wexford Quay in the 1980s, a sad ghost of its former glory. (Rossiter Collection)

dotted with them, perhaps growing with the thirst of the sailors, trawler men and stevedores. This pub is now called the John Barry, but has had a number of incarnations. Situated almost in line with the Raven Point – or Point of the Raven as it should be – across the harbour, it was once called The Raven Bar. Earlier it was Pat Banville's. According to Bassett's Directory, in 1885 there were five licensed premises on Paul Quay, owned by P. Rowe, Catherine Rossiter, Captain M. Devereux, Captain Peter Kearns and P. Lambert. These were probably small premises and would have been secondary income generators, as the two captains were probably still active at sea and Lambert was also listed with a coal yard where he sold coal, culm (what we called slack and used to bank down fires), and salt.

Pierce Court replaces some of what were once the most beautiful buildings on the quays. Here once stood the wonderfully named (though not officially) Penny Dinners. It was earlier occupied by the Sisters of Mercy and they provided cheap wholesome food for the less-well-off people of the town for many years. Here also had been a hat factory in the area.

Stafford's coal yard and offices, and at one time sail lofts, dominated much of Paul Quay, as this section is called. The Paul may refer to a person called Paul Turner or may be from 'Pale', referring to an area adjacent to the old Wexford Castle. The Horse or Bishopswater River flows under Paul Quay into the harbour.

Beyond Oyster Lane was a fine stone warehouse that had been the malt store of Rowe's Mills. The magnificent building on the corner of the Crescent was one of a number of custom houses that served the port at various times. It once boasted a lovely 'belvedere'. This was a small projection from the roof with glass on all sides. From here, the duty officers could observe the harbour and note the arrivals and departures in some comfort.

Turning on to the Crescent we find some of the lovely remnants of old Wexford in a row of slate-fronted houses with beautiful green window shutters. The modern buildings adjacent to these stand on the site of the old Talbot Day and Night Garage. Across Cinema or Harpur's Lane is a series of shops built on the old Stafford's Sawmills site. There, in times past, fine Canadian timber was processed, having been ferried across the Atlantic on Wexford ships.

Crossing Henrietta Street we come to the Ballast Office. This was the headquarters of the Harbour Commissioners and in many ways was the seat of power in the glory days of the port. This once housed the Chamber of Commerce Savings Bank, with trustees R. Sparrow senior, R. Leared, R. Walker, W. Armstrong, W. Browne and W. Timpson.

The rear entrance for Penney's used to boast a fine arch.

Donovan's Wharf is a new construction, the title of which recalls the past. It is built on the site of a variety of businesses ranging from a forge once owned by Mr Browne, who was a veterinary surgeon, to a plumber suppliers that had been Underwood's in the days when such businesses multitasked as shops, cycle agents and undertakers.

Sweeping past the pub incorporated into an old warehouse, we reach another icon of the Crescent in the Bank of Ireland building. Despite a number of changes of use, this has retained its original grandeur and is a fitting reminder of the value that financial institutions put on the port in that they built their bank on the quay.

Cullimore's Lane separates the bank from what was once Murphy's Garage. There is a tale that the rounded roof on Corish's auctioneers came from the United States Naval Airbase at Ferrybank after the Great War. Allen's timber yard occupied this space at one time.

Yet another old bank building, The Provincial, graces the corner of Anne Street, where financial transactions continue under the auspices of Wexford Credit Union. Across the street, on the site where English's opened in 1883 and printed everything from dance tickets to bound books, there are now a number of businesses.

This house on Paul Quay is an example of the use of slate – probably imported by sea from Wales – as weatherproofing on house gables, which appears to have been popular in Wexford in the early twentieth century. (Rossiter Collection)

It is hard to believe that this is the current location of the Bank of Ireland at Custom House Quay. (Courtesy of Kiernan/Scanlon Collection)

SuperValu puts a modern façade where once stood McCormack Brothers, earlier McCormack & Hegarty's. This was a combination hardware, builder suppliers, timber merchants, coal distributor and much more. They imported much of their timber directly by boat, unloading on the quays opposite. Their sign can still be seen in the countryside on haysheds erected by the company.

Another wonderful edifice along here is the old National Bank building, with its sculpted figurehead, one of three banks located on the quay.

After Church Lane there are further new buildings replacing the old.

Keane's building retains some of the stately look of the old quay front, alongside a newly built Bank of Ireland that some recall only as replacing the 1970s monstrosity, but in earlier times this site was occupied by a warehouse. Keane's was built as the Union Club in 1833 and later became the Commercial Club.

Other pubs that stood in this area were Dixie's Lounge and The Kerlogue, commemorating the ship of the same name. The St Iberius Club façade remains, although the club is long gone. Another retained clue to a former glory is the sign for Frank O'Connor's bakery.

Tenders were requested through the *Wexford Independent* of 29 October 1831 for building an office for the Bank of Ireland. *The Wexford Chronicle* dated 24 November 1832 noted, 'The whole Crescent has within a few years founded itself like magic on the waters. Houses, stores and this architectural emporium of wealth are shooting up from the infant sea won foundations.' Since the 1970s it has been an accountant's office and Wexford Borough Council offices. (Rossiter Collection)

Airbase and airship. These photos come from different collections but may refer to the same period during the later months of the Great War, when the United States Navy operated an airbase at Ferrybank.

This picture shows the façade of the old St Iberius Catholic Club in 1982. (Rossiter Collection)

The courthouse was built in 1805 at Commercial Quay. It was designed by R. Morrison according to the *Dublin Almanac* in 1844. Bombs destroyed it on 18 June 1921.

Where Springsteen's and other entertainment venues stand was once the premises of Hugh Maguire, ship chandlers. Maguire had been mayor of Wexford and by coincidence, until expansion by the Centenary Stores, his erstwhile next-door neighbours Kevin Morris and Dominic Kiernan, who ran auctioneering businesses there, were both mayors in later years. The building was used by Breen's Ironmongers in the early twentieth century before being taken over in the mid-1950s by Paddy and Martin McCormack. When Paddy moved down the quay as part of McCormack & Hegarty's and Martin to Gorey, Kevin Morris opened his antique shop and auctioneers business there.

The small building on the corner of Charlotte Street enveloped by the Centenary Stores may be on the site of the old post office. Doyle's plumbers had been located there in the 1900s.

Commercial Quay once had two hotels (again, probably more like guesthouses): The Junction Hotel and The Ship Hotel owned by Green and Sutherland respectively.

The courthouse stood opposite the present bridge until it suffered major damage in June 1921. It had served from the early 1880s.

SOME OF THE SHOPS THAT GRACED MAIN STREET

When researching this section of the book I looked back on the general history of retailing and found some fascinating pieces of information.

As early as 1680, the poor shopkeeper was being lambasted as in this quote from the period, 'Home traders whom we call shopkeepers' add to their own wealth by "buying cheaper and selling dearer".' So, you see, Puritan Britain was not yet a nation of shopkeepers as in the later sense. In fact shopkeeping and working in the trade went through peaks and troughs that we often forget. Shortly after the previous quotation we read that he 'must remember his dependence on the whims of the buyer … we see the best shopkeepers do not think it below them to stand at the door and ask the customers to come in'. The trade of a shop assistant, while never elevated to great heights, did have a need for an apprenticeship. There were various crafts to be learned, and having attained them, the clerk might move on to management or even ownership. Mass production, packaging, and later self-service, would erode all these skills over the decades of the twentieth century.

In 1885, Wexford boasted twenty bakers and flour dealers, seven booksellers and stationers, twenty cattle dealers, six coach builders, four dairies, only two dentists, thirty-two drapers, twelve dressmakers, two emigration agents, five each of fruit and fowl dealers, one gun maker, twelve hardware merchants, seven physicians and surgeons, four printing works, five salt merchants, two ship chandlers, thirteen solicitors, thirty spirit dealers (not including hotels) to only one temperance hall, twenty-four butchers (then called victuallers) and one wine cellar.

In an article in *The Echo* some years back, George Bridges recalled some shops that existed in Selskar in the early 1900s. These included Mrs O'Brien's music shop and Malone's post office, which later became Mulcahy's and is now Xtravision. Billy Malone's vegetable shop often had duck, snipe and rabbit hanging outside. There was Larkin's the bakers, Furlong's butchers and bakers, Mrs Hammond's sweet shop, Meyler's fish shop and Jack Redmond's pig and cattle export business. In the last of these Bridges recalls that there was no rear entrance to the yard so the livestock entered via the front door, down the hall and out the back.

John E. Sinnott, in a letter to *The Echo*, recalled living at 2 South Main Street and that the Dean Art Studios operated by Charles Vize was at the back of the house. He also noted a number of forges that accessed the Main Street during his time. These included one operated by Henry Hogan, just at the top of Coffey's Hill on the left heading north. This may have been associated with a forge by another

Hogan in Batt Street. This was a relatively extensive undertaking and extended up toward Patrick's Square and probably contributed to the name of Foundry Lane, as used for Patrick's Lane.

There appears to have been another forge almost directly opposite, across South Main Street. It was down Henrietta Street behind the current Simon's Place and the old wool shop, when it was Maggie Dempsey's Temperance Hotel. Further south there was yet another forge behind what he recalls as Osbourne's pub but others might remember as The Goal Bar, where Johnny Murphy presided. It is opposite Lowney's.

Hipps was the place for men's suits back in the 1970s. The primary salespeople were Sean Doyle and Jim Dempsey. It was located where Peter Mark now prepares the ladies for those nights out. At one time it was also the front office for *People* Newspapers and earlier still had housed Stamp's Ironmongers and John Sinnott, where you went for furniture, iron and plumbing materials.

This is said to have been one of the first public bath houses in Wexford. We recall it as Dick Whelan's, where he sold newspapers and magazines, cigarettes, cigars and toys. He also repaired umbrellas. In addition there were a ladies and gents hairdressing establishment on the premises. (Courtesy of Kiernan/Scanlon Collection)

The Irish House was a popular store on North Main Street. (Courtesy of Kiernan/Scanlon Collection)

Claire's was once The World of Bennetton, but for many locals it would always be Bessie O'Connor's. There the people who were in for a hard day's shopping would reinvigorate themselves with a fine, hearty home-cooked dinner before braving the roads again. Bessie also sold confectionery. It had been Dixon's drapery shop before her day.

Whelan's newsagents was on the site of the first public bath house in Wexford. In Whelan's time it offered an umbrella-repair service. In earlier days it had been the apothecary shop of Mrs E. Pierce.

Rainbow Valley Boutique was a true child of the flower power generation. I recall that it was started by a group of young people who I recall but will not name – yet. It was upstairs in a building in Oyster Lane. In some ways, the location was a disadvantage as a number of girls are said to have been reluctant to go into a shop run by young lads.

Jack Fane's was a traditional pub-come-grocery shop with a little snug inside the door for the ladies, before the days of equal pub rights. It also had an interesting elevator to the cellar, which was located just inside the door. It was a shop that was very popular with country people and those interested in GAA and horses. A regular patron there was Jackie Culleton, a very well-known dentist who had his practice nearby.

Coffey's was immortalised in a tune by the Boys' Band, or to give them their proper title, St Patrick's Fife and Drum Band. To many Wexford people Coffey's was immortalised in the famous approbation system. We only ever realised that approbation was a word when the sales were on and big signs went up, 'No approbation or credit during the sale.'

Woolworth's came and went in Wexford in less than fifty years. When it was there it was magical. It was a shop with origins in the magical USA. It introduced the idea of limited self-service in many sections – there was always the assistant behind that wide counter. The big thrill was the wide variety of goods on offer under one roof and the amount of gadgets and novelties. Soft whipped ice-cream cornets – we did not get cones – were a great attraction just inside the door. It was there that most of us encountered a '99 when a flake was inserted or had a choice of hundreds and thousands or strawberry syrup on the cornet.

This band has had various names over the years. Officially they are the St Patrick's Fife & Drum Band, but they started as St Bridget's Band and are locally called the Boy's Band. They were always popular with marching groups. (Rossiter Collection)

In 1951, Woolworth's purchased Frank Gaul's shop and premises at 29 South Main Street.
(Kiernan/Scanlon Collection)

Joyce's was established in 1944, and reconstructed in 1960. The China Shop opened 1961 in a former shoe shop. (Courtesy of Kiernan/Scanlon Collection)

Healy & Collins is long gone but the memory of the unique cash system lingers on. It was fascinating to go to this large department store. Buying the goods was incidental to us, but when you paid, the assistant did not go to a cash register. She reached up and unscrewed a thing like a wooden jar and placed the money and a docket inside. This was then screwed back into place. A chain – like the old lavatory chain – was pulled and the container whizzed along on overhead wires to the office. In due time the change arrived back by the same method. I cannot recall the exact engineering of the system but it must have been fantastic.

Sinnott's the chemist was one of many small family chemists in Wexford. People held all chemists in those days in certain awe. Mr Sinnott was a prime example of this. He was well known for concocting his own remedies for many ailments. One that I recall was a cough medicine that had the magical name of 'hippo wine squills' and glycerine. He was later semi-legendary for a lotion that cured aromatic feet.

TVRS was not the first record shop in Wexford but it was a very important step into modern times. They were probably the first shop dedicated solely to music and carrying a wide range of records. The main claim to fame was the introduction of the listening station, where you could listen in private to a record before purchasing. In the past if you wanted to hear a song you had to ask to have it played over the shop system.

Chip shops were an institution before the days of Big Macs and Flame Grilled Whoppers. I will never recall them all but here goes. Nellie Wright's was one of our favourites because it was near to Roche's Terrace, our family outpost. Nellie and Gordon who worked in the shop at the end of Bride Street were conspicuous by their English accents as much as for the lovely chips. Kevin Roche's was on South Main Street and was a popular venue for eating after a night out in the Cinema Palace. It was lovely to sit in at the long tables and eat from enamel plates and hear the film critics in full flow. Peter Dempsey's at Parnell Street provided a similar service for the Capitol Cinema. His specialty was pig's feet and mushy peas. Of course the patrons of The Abbey also had a chipper. For them it was Stamp's in John Street. My main recollection of that establishment was that we went there for our lunch when attending George's Street School.

The name is M. Fox but we knew this as Sheila Fox's, after the hairdressers. The chemist shop to the right is a mystery. It has to be Sinnott's (R.J. Sinnott) but what is the name above it starting with 'The M'? (Courtesy of Kiernan/Scanlon Collection)

Wm Walker & Son was established in 1835 and continued to trade for the next 145 years. The original building was a nice old Georgian type of four storeys. It was demolished in the 1960s to be replaced by the new Walker's, which continued to trade until 1980 when it closed down. They imported most of their goods from source. Everything was done on the premises. Teas were blended, coffee beans were roasted and ground, cheeses were matured, whiskey was racked off (reduced to regulated saleable strength), and all wines, spirits, stout, ales and cordials were prepared, bottled and conditioned in the cellars. The premises was vast in size. The shop had two entrance doors: one from the Main Street and the other on the corner of Charlotte Street. All the shop windows had timber shutters held in place by long iron bars secured with pins from inside the windows and the shop had two counters. The counters and shelving were all solid mahogany which was always kept polished. Stores and lofts were behind the shop, covering a large area towards the quays. The cellars ran from the Main Street more than halfway down Charlotte Street. Other lofts consisted of the tea loft, the cheese loft, dried fruit loft, sweet loft, paper loft, rice loft, jam store, biscuit store, sugar store, bottle store and bottling store, where all Guinness and ales were bottled. A wide array of exotic tinned soups such as pheasant, turtle, bird's nest, fish, turkey, duck, lobster, ox tongue, oyster and royal game were stocked, as well as Valentine's meat juice, calve foot jelly, gentleman's relish and all types of vermicelli, spaghetti, macaroni and rice.

Located at the corner of Oyster Lane, Malone's was a popular fish shop. Note the chopped-off first-floor window indicating that the building was once reduced in height for some reason. (Courtesy of Kiernan/Scanlon Collection)

This fine view of Selskar in the mid-1900s shows Trimmer's Lane, O'Brien's Music Shop, Foley's Provision Store and McCormack's Chemist's. The chemist was said to be located in a building once owned by George Bernard Shaw. (Courtesy of Kiernan/Scanlon Collection)

Above: The closing of McCormack's marked the end of another Wexford era. (Rossiter Collection)

Left: Apart from the unusual finish on the top of the building here, Paddy Lyon's is said to have one other claim to fame. It is said that this shoe shop was the first in Wexford to issue plastic carrier bags with the name of the shop printed on them. (Rossiter Collection)

BITS

This chapter will be the repository for those pieces of memory too important to forget but not long enough to merit a chapter of their own. It might make an interesting pub-quiz round.

CARNIVAL

Today we have funfairs, but when I was growing up these were called carnivals and Wexford had a few fields that were known as 'The Carnival Fields'. The proper names of the fields were Harvey's (accessed from Talbot Street) and Kirwan's (that opened on to Carrigeen). There were others, such as Red Pat's in George's Street, but that was before my time.

The carnival was usually a family affair, such as McFadden's or McCauley's. McFadden's Hippodrome was advertised as being at Carrigeen in 1953. They were not huge, thrill-making affairs in those days. The most fear-inducing rides were the chair planes or the swing boats. For the younger reader, the chair planes were more chair than plane. This machine was a large rotating construction with a number of seats suspended by chains. As the contraption rotated, the chairs swung out over the crowd. The swing boats were a sort of boat suspended from a cross beam. It held two or four people and as the name suggests it swung back and forth. These were the main teenage attractions.

There were also the usual children's rides such as the roundabout. When these had horses that looked like they were going up and down as well they were referred to as 'hobby horses' for some reason. In other countries, that referred to the wooden horse's head that children pretended to ride. It might also be known as the merry-go-round.

The adults usually had carnival fun with trying to win a goldfish on the rifle range – these fish usually died within days. You could also win a prize by throwing rings over boxes. One of my favourites was 'roll a penny'. In this, you rolled a penny down a chute and tried to get it to land in a square. If it stopped neatly inside the lines you won the equivalent of the number in pennies. I wonder if that made us 'high rollers' like in Las Vegas?

We didn't have the coconut shy as seen in so many comics of the time but we did try to knock down cans with tennis balls. Many of the carnival games would migrate to the ubiquitous parish field days.

BERNADETTE PLACE

This estate, leading off The Faythe, was blessed and opened in September 1958.

THE BOOK CENTRE

This first opened beside Hassett's, in what had earlier been Forte's and before that The Tip Top. It was officially opened by Frank Hall, who was at the peak of popularity with *Hall's Pictorial Weekly*, on 13 June 1975. The author Eilish Dillon made a book signing appearance there 16 June.

BUS SERVICE

Before the current Shuttle Bus, Wexford was deemed too small for a regular bus service. But in 1962 the North End Development Association had organised a regular suburban bus service, bringing shoppers from Maudlintown, Bishopswater, Corish Park and other such frontier outposts to the north end of town to do business. They carried 900 passengers on the first day.

CREDIT UNION

The Wexford branch of the Credit Union began with a meeting in the Dun Mhuire in 1962. The offices were later in the Bullring, in a small premises that would later become the first of our many discount stores, the Poundstretcher. This shop was opened by Arthur Kelly and had a mural of a pound note that I think was painted by Tony Robinson, then a community artist at Wexford Arts Centre.

FUNERALS

Sunday funerals ended in Wexford 1975.

ONE-WAY TRAFFIC

This was first proposed for Wexford's narrow streets in 1963.

Cattle Mart. In days gone by there were fairs and markets in various parts of the town. The cattle sales moved to Hill Street and eventually settled at Redmond Road. These are some of the pens used for holding the animals. (Rossiter Collection)

PINEWOOD ESTATE

In 1970, the show house was declared open, with three-bedroom houses on offer from £3,950.00.

PRICES

In 1962, a bottle of stout cost 11*d*, with the large bottle at 1*s* 7*d*. Whiskey was 4*s* 4*d* a glass and lager 1*s* 6*d* a pint. Dancing to The Majestic Showband would cost you 5*s*. In 1977, postage stamps were 10p first class and 8p second. A local phone call cost 4p. In 1967, the Strand Hotel, Rosslare offered a sauna, swim and massage for £1. You could swim in the heated pool for 4*s* and dinner and a dance cost £1 1*s*. In 1972, the cover price of *The People* went from 5p to 6p

Burton's was part of a huge chain that covered the British Isles in the middle of the twentieth century. Their tailoring clothed many a groom in its day. The shop on the corner of Rowe Street is Breen's. (Courtesy of Kiernan/Scanlon Collection)

RENAULT 8

The first Wexford-assembled Renault 8 motor car drove through the factory gates at Trinity Street on Tuesday 23 November 1964.

SAUNA

The first public sauna in Wexford was introduced at John North's barbers shop in King Street in 1970.

SCHOOL

The roof of an extension in the CBS school in Thomas Street collapsed at 10.45p.m. in December 1970.

TURNOVER TAX

In 1963, Turnover Tax, the forerunner of VAT, was introduced.

The Arts Centre was originally built as the Assembly Rooms and the Market House in 1775. Over the centuries the building had a number of uses. The Brunswick Club for Protestants was founded here in 1828, and later the Volunteers also held meetings here. It was the Town Hall until the mid-1940s and there was a very popular ballroom in the building in the 1940s and 1950s. It became the Arts Centre in 1974. (Courtesy of Kiernan/Scanlon Collection)

Bottom of George's Street.

PUBS

In 1962, The Phoenix Bar, St Aidan's Crescent, advertised itself as 'the most luxurious outside the hotels'.

SOCIAL WELFARE PAYMENTS

In 1971, unemployment assistance for a single person was £3 12s; with an adult dependant it was £6 8s and a couple with one child got £7 3s. By 1977, these figures had risen to £9.80 single, £17.05 for an adult dependant, and £20.20 for a couple with one child. Children's allowance was £2.30 per month per child.

ST AIDAN'S SHOPPING CENTRE

This out-of-town shopping centre opened on 6 February 1970 at 10.30a.m.

TRAFFIC CHAOS

In January 1967, there was mayhem when a ninety-seven-ton transformer bound for Great Island on a trailer pulled by two trucks crossed the bridge. Traffic stopped, two cars crashed, and two cows ran along the Woodenworks.

CLOSED

Wexford Harbour was officially declared closed due to the sandbar at its mouth in 1963.

WORK

In 1965, the banks began working a five-day week. Shop workers sought a five-day week in January 1969.

The Woodenworks, or Pilewharf, were erected in the 1880s to allow railway wagons to be loaded and unloaded with cargoes from the Wexford ships which plied the oceans of the world, from Odessa to Savannah. (Rossiter Collection)

TELEPHONE

Today we have flip phones, iPhones and all classes of gadgets, but who recalls the A and B phones? We are not going back to Alexander Graham Bell, but to the 1950s through to the 1970s. That was a time of few house phones, so we relied on those in shops or the few public telephone kiosks – green and cream with small window panes. There was an art to using such telephones and they also employed the services of a telephone operator.

Above left: Now mostly derelict and waiting for development, the piece of old Wexford protruding into the harbour at Trinity Street was once a hive of activity, with various industrial enterprises located there over the years. This picture shows that a version of the Woodenworks once skirted the reclaimed embankment. (Rossiter Collection)

Above right: The original Walkers was an old Georgian building of four storeys. It was demolished in the sixties to be replaced by the new Walkers, which continued to trade until 1980. The one shop which was Walkers now houses six shops and is known as Walkers Mall. Many people will remember the smell of roasting coffee beans wafting up Main Street from Walkers. (Rossiter Collection)

Westlands.

You had to insert your money in the slot to activate the phone. Then, if it was a local call, you could dial the number. When the person answered you pressed button 'A' and with luck you got connected. If there was no reply, button 'B' returned your money. This worked, unless some gurrier had stuffed paper in the chute so you assumed a faulty mechanism and left the money for him or her to retrieve.

If it was a long-distance or trunk call, you needed operator assistance and he or she gave instructions on pressing the button. You needed deep pockets of change for any long conversation with distant friends, as the operator came on every few minutes requesting more money in the slot.

SELSKAR ABBEY

When the owner of Walkers, John Henry Martin died in the early 1950s, his was the last funeral to leave Selskar Abbey before it was de-roofed.

THE PAST IS ALIVE

This is the final book of the latest quartet on Wexford Town and this section is being used to show that a genuine interest in the past of this 'ancient and historic borough' is still evident. In earlier books, I asked people to comment or to add to the store of knowledge being published. There was not exactly a deluge of information but a number of people did take the time to stop me and comment. Here we distil the essence of this added wisdom.

I met a man in old *Still Lane* who spoke of having lived in Oyster Lane. The house was just down a little from Main Street on the south side. It was big – four rooms up and four down with a door which may have led to another section. Could this have been a tavern? He used to help Swanker Malone with cooperage after school. The coopers was at the present store on south side. He remembers four or five houses occupied. One was at sea end. His son had a rissole making business in Carney's Lane in John Street. This was approaching the slaughterhouse beside O'Byrne's. In later times, letters were addressed to Carnew's Lane. This may be a slip of the pen.

This view of the Vallotin Monument at Wygram shows how this road looked about a half century ago. (Kiernan/Scanlon Collection)

Going to the spout was a common requirement in the middle and early twentieth century. There were public spouts for water in most areas like this one at the Rocks Road or Mulgannon. (Courtesy of Kiernan/Scanlon Collection)

Furlong's Lane was in Bride Street – where The Cabinet Shop is today. I found this on an old Griffith's Valuation map.

Kearney's Lane was located at John's Street until the 1970s. It was almost opposite John's Gate Street and Eamon Doyle mentioned that there was a slaughterhouse and two dwellings in the lane that he thinks were occupied by Mernaghs and Recks.

John Street, according to Eamon Doyle, had three 'houses with huckster shops' between the current Traynors and Kearney's Lane. They were occupied by Clooneys, Hagans and Ffrenches.

Here is another relic of times long gone. This signal box was at the South Station, staging post for the regular Sunday excursions to Rosslare Strand. In those days there were manned signal boxes at all railway stations, with big heavy levers to be pulled to clear the way onto the relevant tracks. The signal box was also the location for a popular television comedy show in the 1960s, with Jimmy O'Dea and Frank Kelly philosophising every Sunday night.

This picture, taken in the latter days of the old Woodenworks, reminds us of the working quays when machinery like this was used to open sections of the Crescent to allow boats access. (Rossiter Collection)

Dr Toddy Pierse's son response to an earlier publication reminded me that his great-grandfather Dr James Pierse was the first with the surname with an 's' in Wexford. He hailed from Listowel and qualified as a doctor in 1829. He arrived in Wexford in 1836.

King Street Eamon Doyle informs me that The Pillar development on the old malthouse site refers back to a sixteenth-century inn called The Golden Pillar that stood on the site beside the Bishopswater River.

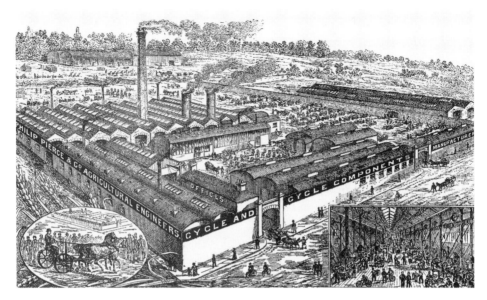

This is a fascinating artist's rendition of what the Pierce Foundry looked like in the late 1800s – its heyday.

Here we see a sad picture of an industrial past that would not recover. After more than a century of employing large numbers of Wexford men and women, in 2004 Pierce's had closed and was a slowly being demolished behind its walls. (Rossiter Collection)

MY WEXFORD (NONSUCH PUBLISHING, 2006)

John E. Sinnott provided some fresh information on Wexford as a result of this publication. The Theatre Royal sign that stood on South Main Street was attached to his family home and the use of the sign permitted the family free entry to the theatre.

He recalls Bob Doyle, who had a sweet factory in the area in the mid-twentieth century.

The building around number 2 South Main Street had belonged to Haddens of Wygram in the 1700s.

Anne Street had The Wexford Club, which was also known as The Gentlemen's Club.

STREETS OF WEXFORD (THE HISTORY PRESS IRELAND, 2009)

The following came from Jim Bergin by email:

Looking at the photo of Green Street on the left-hand pavement, there is a trickle of water running to the gutter. This is from a tap fixed to the wall. This tap served as the water supply to the first few houses on the right, including our house, No.2, as we did not have running water. If this tap stopped working for whatever reason, we had to fetch the water from a well at the top of the street near to Bailey's pub.

I remember when children came out of the CBS school and played around with the tap, a widow, all in black, used to chase them off waiving a walking stick. Who she was or which house she lived in I can't recall. I do recall a Brother Cullen who seemed to be involved with the sports at the CBS.

Before he came to England (in 1942), my father Dan Bergin was a barber who worked from the front room of my grandmother's house in Carrigeen. This house was occupied until a few years ago by my uncle, another Jim Bergin. My father learnt his trade from my great-uncle Mylie Bergin, who had his barber's shop in Gibson's Lane. My father and my uncle Jim were members of the fife and drum band that were runners-up in an All-Ireland band competition in 1926.

Thank you all for taking the time to add these extra nuggets to the rich and varied history of Wexford. They may seem trivial but it is this accumulation of facts and stories that will inform generations to come.

If you have other information to add, please email me at stories@iol.ie and I will find some way of recording it for posterity You may add your thoughts, criticisms, picture and stories to our Facebook page, Remebering Wexford.

BIBLIOGRAPHY

BOOKS

Basset, *Wexford County Guide & Directory* (Dublin, 1885).

Colfer, B., *Wexford, a Town and its Landscape* (Cork: Cork University Press 2008).

Enright, Michael, *Men of Iron* (Wexford, 1987).

Griffith, G., *Chronicles of County Wexford* (Enniscorthy, 1877).

Griffith's Valuations.

Hore, P.H., *History of Town and County of Wexford – 1906* (reprinted Professional Books, 1979).

Horn, Pamela, *Behind the Counter* (Sutton Publishing, 2006).

Jenkins, Jim, *The Port & Quays of Wexford* (2001).

Jenkins, Jim, *Retailing in Wexford 1930 to 1990* (1996).

Kehoe, M.T., *Wexford – Its Streets and People* (n.d.).

Lacy, T., *Sights and Scenes in Our Fatherland* (London, 1863).

Ranson, J., *Songs of the Wexford Coast* (Wexford, 1975).

Reck, P. *Wexford – A Municipal History* (Mulgannon Publications, 1987).

Roche, Rossiter, Hurley & Hayes, *Walk Wexford Ways* (1988).

Rossiter, Hurley, Roche & Hayes, *A Wexford Miscellany* (WHP, 1994).

Rossiter, N., *Wexford Port* (WCTU, 1989).

Rossiter, N., *My Wexford* (Dublin: Nonsuch/The History Press Ireland, 2006).

Rossiter, N., *Wexford, a history, a tour, a miscellany* (Dublin: Nonsuch/The History Press Ireland, 2005).

Rowe & Scallan, *Houses of Wexford* (Ballinakella Press, 2004).

NEWSPAPERS

The Free Press
Walsh, Dan, 'In Our Time', *The Echo*
The Wexford People
Wexford Echo
Wexford Independent
Wexford Herald

JOURNALS

Journal of the Wexford Historical Society, various articles.
The Past, various articles.

PERSONAL NOTES/UNPUBLISHED RESEARCH

Bergin, Jim – correspondence
Doyle, Eamon
Gaul, Liam
O'Connor Sylvia, *The Baker's Dozen* (unpublished).
O'Leary, Jack
Pierce, James
Sinnott, John E.
Wickham Peterson, Brenda – correspondence